# LIFT OFF!

## KEY SKILLS IN ENGLISH

### Janna Tiearney

# Fifth Class

## Activity Book

Carroll
Education
Limited

# Introduction to Teachers and Parents

This book is one of a series of English Skills Books aimed at children in First to Sixth Class: 1, 2, 3, 4, 5 and 6. The *Lift Off!* series has been written by an experienced primary school teacher, Janna Tiearney who has devised a specific scheme of work on the teaching of core English skills in direct response to feedback from teachers around the country.

## How to use this book

This book is self-contained and designed to be used independently by children alongside any core English programme. This book is laid out in a child-friendly manner and includes contemporary and engaging artwork and themes. The reading texts and exercises have been carefully graded and each book is a continuation and revision of the content of the previous book. The earlier books naturally place a greater emphasis on word sounds and phonics, while the later books focus more on grammar. All books contain a consistent format of activities to promote children's confidence. Each unit covers all three strands of the English curriculum: reading, writing and oral language. Each unit, in each book, consists of 6 pages. Each page carries its own *Friendly Owl* icon in the top corner of the page.

| Page | Icon | | Content |
|------|------|--|---------|
| Page 1 | | Reading | Pre-reading question, illustration and reading text |
| Page 2 | | Reading & responding | 'Talk about' topic, comprehension and higher order questions |
| Page 3 | | Sounds | Letter sounds and phonics activities using visual support |
| Page 4 | | Grammar | Activities including rules, examples, drill and practice questions |
| Page 5 | | Looking at words | Spelling activities using sight words from the reading section |
| Page 6 | | Extra optional page | Optional drama, personal writing and a fun puzzle section |

## Other features

- **'Before you read ...'** question: will capture the child's interest and give him/her a purpose for reading.
- **'Talk about'** oral language activities follow each reading piece encouraging children to engage fully with the text and create their own meaning.
- **Information bubbles** are dotted throughout the book for the purpose of fun, as points of information and to promote further thinking on the theme or given concept.
- **'Remember boxes'** are used throughout the grammar sections to assess and remind children of what they have learned already.
- **'Sample boxes'** provide the children with important, accessible examples to ensure they understand the grammar point before completing the task.
- **Revision pages** appear at key stages in the book to promote the revisiting and consolidation of letter sounds and crucial grammar points and as a means of assessing progress during the year.
- **Integrated activities within each unit:** The personal writing, sight words, and oral language activities are linked to the reading text. This means that the children are familiar with the topic by the time they come to write about it.
- **Comprehensive sight word list:** Each unit has a list of sight words that children can read in context. By completing the sight word activities in each unit, children are able to build up a comprehensive list of sight words, which they can then use in their own writing and reading.
- **Effective spelling strategies:** The 'Looking at words' page uses the *Look and say, picture, cover, write and check* method to teach spellings. A word list is provided and there are spaces to record the spellings and more spaces to correct any spelling mistakes. Other word recognition strategies have been included to encourage children to find the strategies that work best for them.

# Fifth Class Activity Book
# Contents

Do you know where Mexico is?

1. Read the story.

## The holes of Lagos – a tale from Mexico

One fine morning, the mayor of Lagos, in Mexico, crossed the market square. There he found a deep hole. He stopped, looked at the hole and said to himself, 'This hole is dangerous! Someone could fall in! Who put this hole here?'

No-one seemed to know who had made the hole. The mayor called the policeman, Carlos.
'This hole must be filled at once!' said the mayor.
'Si Senõr, it will be done right away,' said Carlos.

Carlos called all the men of Lagos together. They began digging up the earth from a place nearby, and threw it into the hole. The sun was hot and the men wore sombreros to protect their faces. Soon, the hole was filled and the mayor was pleased.
'We have good men in our town,' he said.

The mayor walked on and came across another deep hole. This was where the earth had been taken to fill the first hole. 'Carlos!' he called. 'Here is another hole! This must be filled first thing tomorrow.'
'Si, Senõr, it will be done,' said Carlos.

So the next day the men of Lagos dug up more earth to fill the new hole. The mayor came to watch the men at work and he was pleased and proud of the men. Soon the second hole was filled and everyone was relieved.

The mayor walked on. He hadn't walked far when he saw another hole! 'Carlos!' he yelled. 'There is another hole! Holes grow in Lagos like weeds in a cornfield. This dangerous hole must be filled in the morning.'
'Si, Senõr, it will be done,' said Carlos.

This went on and on. People in the town could not understand it. So they kept on filling holes by digging new ones until they came to the edge of the town.

The people in the next town had been watching the men of Lagos day by day. They were laughing to themselves but they said nothing. When the hole was next to their town, they quietly filled it with rubbish and covered it with sand.
The mayor of Lagos saw the last hole filled and could not find another. He was overjoyed.
'The men of this town never give up until a job is finished,' he said.

The men of Lagos were pleased too as they were getting tired of so much digging every day. At last, there were no more holes in Lagos and everyone was happy.

Mexican food includes tacos and enchiladas.

A sombrero is a broad-brimmed hat made of straw or felt.

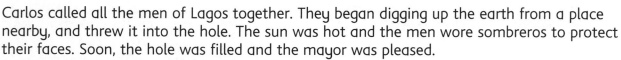

2. Talk about.

Say these Spanish words. Practise them until you know them off by heart.

a.   hola (hello)
b.   adios (goodbye)
c.   commo estas (how are you?)
d.   felice anos (happy birthday)
e.   felice Navidad (happy Christmas)

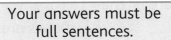

Your answers must be full sentences.

3. Answer the questions in your copybook.

a.   Who found the first hole?
b.   Where was the hole?
c.   Who is Carlos?
d.   How was the first hole filled?
e.   Who was filling the holes?
f.   How did more holes appear?
g.   What did the people in the next town do?

4. Answer the questions in your copybook.

a.   What was the weather like?
b.   Why was the mayor concerned?
c.   How do you think the mayor felt when the holes kept appearing?
d.   What did the mayor think of the men?
e.   How do you think the first hole might have been created?

5. Find words in the story with the same meaning. Use your dictionary to look up words you do not know.

a.   a person who enforces the law    _____
b.   soil    _____
c.   the day after today    _____
d.   observing    _____
e.   garbage    _____
f.   weary    _____

6. Write your own sentence using one or more of the words from question five.

_____

_____.

The word **there** means in that place.

> Sample The class has been **there** before.

It is also used with the verb **to be**.

> Sample **There** is a badger in my garden.

The word **their** means **belonging to them**. It is always followed by a noun.

> Sample I wish **their** dog would stop digging in my flowers.

7. Write **there** or **their** to complete the sentences. Rewrite the sentences in your copybook.

   a. _____ friends are over _____ in the field.

   b. _____ and then, the teacher took away _____ mobile phones.

   c. _____ car is old, but _____ tractor is new.

   d. The robins built _____ nests _____ last year.

   e. _____ is a high fence right around _____ property.

   f. _____ English books are _____ on the teacher's desk.

   g. _____ are no naughty children _____.

   h. I sat _____ watching the birds eating _____ seeds.

   i. It is _____ dogs that keep me awake at night with _____ barking.

   j. _____ was no sign of the teachers or _____ classes.

The word **where** is used for places or positions.

> Sample This is the place **where** we learn.

The word **were** is the past tense of the word **are**.

> Sample The children **were** studying hard for their test.

The word **wear** is what you do with your clothes or jewellery.

> Sample Please do not **wear** your cap in the classroom.

> You cannot **wear** that in a place **where** you learn!

8. Write **where**, **were** or **wear** to complete the sentences. Rewrite the sentences in your copybook.

   a. That is the school _____ you don't have to _____ a uniform.

   b. If you _____ that floppy hat, you won't be able to see _____ you are going.

   c. The children _____ playing _____ the parents could see them.

   d. The classes _____ going on an outing and they had to _____ old clothes.

   e. If you _____ me, what would you _____ to the disco?

   f. The teachers _____ discussing _____ we could play the match.

   g. I do not know _____ Mum put the CD we _____ listening to.

   h. The days _____ sunny and so the children did not need to _____ warm clothing.

We use capital letters:
- At the beginning of a sentence
- For the pronoun I
- For the names and titles of people, such as, Miss Jelly Bean
- For the names of places, months, days of the week, special days, mountains and rivers.
- Sentences end with a full stop, question mark or exclamation mark.

9. Add capital letters, full stops and question marks to these sentences. Rewrite them correctly in your copybook.

   a. the 14ᵗʰ february is st valentine's day
   b. last sunday I visited my aunt penelope
   c. the rte channel has irish programmes
   d. i wish i could live in the white house with the president
   e. mr white flies to spain each july to get a tan
   f. i really want a puppy for my birthday in april
   g. mr bean asked miss sprout to go on a date on saturday
   h. may i join you for lunch at tommy's tavern
   i. lucy loves dancing to elvis presley's music
   j. kim and brian will climb mount kilimanjaro in january

On St. Patrick's Day, I will be a leprechaun.

10. Rewrite this paragraph in your copybook, adding capital letters, full stops and question marks.

   what man-made structures can be seen from the moon the answer is none some people believe you can see the great wall of china from the moon but this is untrue quite a few things can be seen from space because 'space' is quite close it starts about 60km from the earth's surface things that can be seen are motorways, ships on the sea, railways, cities and even some buildings from the moon, which is about 400,000km away, it is difficult to even make out the continents

Capital letters are also used for titles of movies, plays and books.

> **Sample** Kimmy loves the film *Princess Diaries*.

Sometimes titles are written in italics.

11. Underline the titles. Rewrite the sentences correctly in your copybook, adding capital letters, full stops and question marks.

   a. i am reading a book by roald dahl called charlie and the chocolate factory
   b. have you read the book called under the hawthorn tree
   c. the play hamlet by shakespeare was exciting to watch
   d. i think the movie shrek is better than the movie the lion king
   e. the pantomime in dublin this year is called the snow goose
   f. my dad enjoys reading the farmer's weekly
   g. the poem mid term break was written by seamus heaney
   h. the giggler treatment is a book by irish author roddy doyle

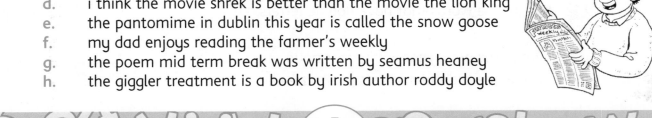

**Word list**

| | | | | |
|---|---|---|---|---|
| mayor | Mexico | protect | across | tomorrow |
| themselves | rubbish | understand | finished | square |

12. Learn the spellings. Now look and say, picture, cover, write, check.

_____     _____

_____     _____

_____     _____

_____     _____

13. Write any words you got wrong.

_____

14. Fill in the missing words. Use the word list.

   a.   In _____ the people speak Spanish.

   b.   I think I will do my homework _____.

   c.   We walked _____ the bridge to get to the match.

   d.   Wear sunglasses in summer to _____ your eyes.

   e.   A _____ is a four-sided shape.

> Protect yourself when skateboarding.

15. In your copybook write your own sentences using these words:
   **mayor**, **rubbish**, **finished**, **themselves** and **understand**.

16. Write the answers. Use the word list.

   a.   Break **understand** into two words. _____  _____

   b.   Break these words into syllables. Write the number of syllables for each.
   **tomorrow** _____ **mayor** _____ **rubbish** _____ **Mexico** _____

   c.   Find three smaller words in the word **finished**.

   _____  _____  _____

   d.   Which words from the list end with these?

   **or** _____   **row** _____   **are** _____

   e.   Write the first five words from the list in alphabetical order.

   _____  _____  _____

   _____  _____

   f.   Write the words that have double letters.

   _____  _____  _____

   g.   Write the word that is a proper noun. _____

   h.   Underline the silent letters in **square**.

## Talk about

17. Work in groups. Act out the story of *The holes of Lagos*.
There will be roles for the mayor, Carlos, the working men and
people from the other town.

## Write about

Making a summary means writing down the main points only. You still need to write
full sentences. Underlining KEY WORDS may help you when you write your summary.

18. Summarise the following sentences.

 a. The full bright moon hung in the black night sky.

 _____

 b. The old rusty car struggled to make it up the steep hill as it spluttered and
 choked its way along.

 _____

19. In your copybook write a summary of the story *The holes of Lagos*.

Primary school in Mexico is called Primaria.

20. What are these pictograms saying?

 a. MCE MCE MCE

 c. **PEN** sword

 e. **M1LLION**

 b. G H O R S I N (arranged in circle)

 d. **go it it it it**

 f. GOOD BE TRUE / GOOD BE TRUE

 a. _____

 b. _____

 c. _____

 d. _____

 e. _____

 f. _____

Have you ever seen a sloth?

1. Read the information.

## Sloths

The sloth is an animal that lives in South America where it spends most of its time hanging upside-down in trees. The sloth has powerful, curved claws to hold onto the branches. It gives birth, eats and sleeps hanging upside-down! It spends 15-18 hours asleep each day. An animal that spends most of its life in a tree is called arboreal.

Hoffmann's Two-toed Sloth

The sloth's fur, which can be brown or grey in colour, grows in the opposite direction to that of most animals. It points towards the ground so that rain runs off its body. Size and weight differ, for example, the Maned three-toed sloth weighs about 5kg and the Hoffman's Two-toed sloth weighs about 60kg. The sloth has a short, flat head, big eyes, a short snout, long legs and tiny ears. It has an amazing ability to heal itself and its wounds hardly ever become infected.

A sloth eats mostly leaves. A meal can be kept in the digestive system for over a month. It may also eat insects and small lizards.

A sloth moves very slowly. On land, it can only move in an awkward crawl because of its long claws. Algae grow in the grooves on a sloth's fur and this helps to camouflage it in the forest greenery. On the ground the maximum speed is 1.5 metres per minute. They mostly move at less than 30 centimetres per minute.

The mother sloth carries her young for up to nine months on her belly, where it feeds on the leaves it can reach. A female sloth will usually have one offspring per year.

The sloth's main predators are the harpy eagle, humans and the jaguar.

The two-toed sloth and the tree-toed sloth both have three toes on each foot! The two-toed sloth has only two fingers.

A sloth does not do well in captivity as it cannot fight diseases very well.

2. Talk about.

What other strange creatures do you know? Perform a mime of a strange creature for the class to guess.
Try to walk as slowly as the sloth!

3. Answer the questions.

a. Where does the sloth live? _____

b. Describe how it moves. _____
_____

c. How is the sloth's fur different to that of other animals? _____
_____

d. What does a sloth eat? _____

e. For how long does the mother carry the infant? _____

f. Name a creature that may prey on a sloth. _____

4. Complete the sentences in this paragraph.

The sloth holds onto branches with its curved and _____ claws. It _____ for about 15–18 hours each day. The sloth is _____ to heal itself and hardly ever gets infections. It eats mostly leaves and a meal can _____ in the digestive system for more than a month. It is well _____ because of the green algae that grows on its fur. A _____ sloth will usually have one offspring annually.

5. Write the meanings of these words in context. Use your dictionary.

a. arboreal _____

b. wounds _____

c. awkward _____

d. camouflage _____

e. offspring _____

f. predators _____

> **In context** means you need to look at the word in the text and write its meaning as it is used in the text.

6. Answer the questions in your copybook.

a. Describe what the sloth looks like.

b. Do you think they would be easy to spot in the wild? Give a reason for your answer.

c. How are they adapted to living in trees?

d. What do you think is interesting about the sloth?

Homophones are words that sound the same but have different spellings and meanings.

> **Sample** I can **see** a ship far out to **sea**.

7.  Find a word that sounds the same but has a different meaning and spelling.

| | | | | | |
|---|---|---|---|---|---|
| a. | tale | _____ | g. | won | _____ |
| b. | know | _____ | h. | sew | _____ |
| c. | right | _____ | i. | made | _____ |
| d. | our | _____ | j. | wood | _____ |
| e. | sail | _____ | k. | son | _____ |
| f. | eight | _____ | l. | bare | _____ |

8.  Circle the correct word. Rewrite the sentences in your copybook.

a.  May I have another (piece / peace) of pizza?
b.  I am going to buy a new (pear / pair) of hiking boots.
c.  The (witch / which) had a bubbling cauldron.
d.  Can you (here / hear) the teacher laughing?
e.  The bird was perched on the (bow / bough) of the tree.
f.  You should not play in the building (sight / site).
g.  The (bridal / bridle) party smiled for the photographs.
h.  I like the (yoke / yolk) of my egg to be runny.
i.  During the race, he pulled a (mussel / muscle) in his leg.
j.  The telephone (chord / cord) is tangled.

How much longer do **I need** to **knead** this bread?

9.  Write sentences using each pair of homophones. Do not worry if they are silly!

a.  road / rode _____
b.  missed / mist _____
c.  you / ewe _____
d.  raw / roar _____
e.  flour / flower _____
f.  steal / steel _____
g.  pail / pale _____
h.  maid / made _____
i.  horse / hoarse _____
j.  we'll / wheel _____

My brother breaks the brakes on this thing!

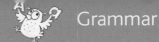

**Remember:** Commas are used in lists.

> **Sample** For breakfast I want toast, cereal, eggs, bacon, sausages and fruit.

10. Add commas. Rewrite the sentences in your copybook.

    a. On my desk there is a ruler a pen a crayon and an orange.
    b. Mandy Luke Jimmy and Jess are my friends.
    c. I like lettuce cucumber tomato sardines and pepper on my sandwich.
    d. The types of music I like are reggae rock dance and pop.
    e. On the farm we have cows sheep turkeys pigs ducks geese and chickens.
    f. You can have tea coffee cocoa milk orange juice or water.
    g. Before you start eating make sure you have a knife fork spoon and napkin.
    h. At our school you can take part in tennis football hurley cricket swimming drama music and art.
    i. I think aliens have long fingers curly ears green skin blue teeth no hair big stomachs and black antennae.
    j. For dinner my friend offered me ham sandwiches mouldy potatoes strawberry yoghurt garlic cabbage fairy cakes or cheesy rice.

Commas are used to show pauses in a sentence, making it easier to read.

> **Sample** After the teacher left, the children started talking.

11. Add commas. Rewrite the sentences in your copybook.

    a. Annie loves broccoli but she won't eat spinach.
    b. Henry wanted to ride a horse especially a Shetland.
    c. After Mum and Dad left we threw a party.
    d. Burt's bike had been stolen so he couldn't get to school.
    e. When the teacher leaves the room let's try to be good.
    f. He ran for the bus but he was too late.
    g. The child begged for more sweets but everyone ignored him.
    h. After baking blueberry muffins we had to clean up the kitchen.
    i. I wanted to go to the party but I was just too tired.
    j. When the teacher comes back we will all pretend we have been working.

12. Add capital letters, commas and full stops. Rewrite the sentences correctly in your copybook.

    a. although kim was happy with the gift she really wanted a football new runners and a ticket to see manchester united
    b. mark and orla are going to australia new zealand and thailand
    c. our teacher mr. moody wanted to take the class to see the play romeo and juliet
    d. because my brother tim has been so good mum is taking him to the movies to see king kong
    e. my cat ginger likes to sleep on my bed but he keeps me awake with his purring
    f. the sun was shining on saturday but it was still cold

**Word list**

| sloth | weight | curved | opposite | awkward |
| system | towards | crawl | usually | humans |

13. Learn the spellings. Now look and say, picture, cover, write, check.

_____    _____
_____    _____
_____    _____
_____    _____
_____    _____

14. Write any words you got wrong.

_____

15. Fill in the missing words. Use the word list.

    a.    Sometimes I feel _____ when I have to give a talk.

    b.    A baby will _____ before she can walk.

    c.    Our family _____ eats a roast dinner on Sundays.

    d.    The _____ of my schoolbag gives me backache.

    e.    The _____ of asleep is awake.

Are they humans?

16. In your copybook write your own sentences using these words:
**sloth**, **curved**, **system**, **towards** and **humans**.

17. Write the answers. Use the word list.

    a.    Which words from the list end with these words?

        **site** _____ **stem** _____ **wards** _____

    b.    Find smaller words in these words:

        **sloth** _____ **usually** _____ **humans** _____ **crawl** _____

    c.    Write one word in plural form. _____

    d.    Write the root words.

        **usually** _____ **curved** _____

    e.    Underline a letter pattern that is the same in each word:

        **awkward    towards**

    f.    Break these words into syllables. Write the number of syllables for each.

        **opposite** _____ **towards** _____

        **crawl** _____ **usually** _____

    g.    Change one letter in each word to make words from the list:

        **carved** _____ **humane** _____

    h.    Write one noun from the word list. _____

**Talk about**

18. Work in pairs. Tell each other what you have learnt about the sloth.
Read this poem together.

### The sloth

In moving-slow he has no Peer.
You ask him something in his Ear,
He thinks about it for a Year;

And, then, before he says a Word
There, upside down (unlike a Bird),
He will assume that you have Heard—

A most Ex-as-per-at-ing Lug.
But should you call his manner Smug,
He'll sigh and give his Branch a Hug;

Then off again to Sleep he goes,
Still swaying gently by his Toes,
And you just know he knows he knows.

*Theodore Roethke*

19. Complete the information table. When writing a table you do not need to write full sentences!

| The sloth | |
|---|---|
| Country | |
| Habitat | |
| Appearance | |
| Diet | |
| Enemies | |
| Speed | |
| Sleep pattern | |
| An interesting fact | |

20. Research an animal that interests you. In your copybook use the same table to write facts about the animal.

21. Unscramble the letters to find the names of wild animals.

a. pirat     t__ __ir
b. kardaarv     aa__ __ __ __ __ __
c. noobab     b__ __ __ __n
d. seomo     m__ __ __ __
e. rumel     l__ __ __ __

f. wobtam     w__ m__ __ __
g. kel     __ __k
h. bonbig     g__b__ __n
i. yenha     h__ __ __ __a
j. mipknuch     __ __ip__ __ __k

What do you do on Saturday mornings?
1.   Read the poem.

## Saturday morning where I live

My brothers are two happy little boys,
And five years old – and twins. That's twice the noise.
My sister plays CDs, and she annoys
My Mum with the loud music she enjoys.

The dog licks out his bowl and barks for more.
My Dad stuffs washing in and slams the door,
And sets our old machine to shake and roar;
It spills his cornflakes on the kitchen floor.

The tv's on, of course, and someone's trying
To sell us things we'd never dream of buying,
And that starts up the neighbours' baby crying
– *And now our shirts and pants are tumble-drying – !*

But then, quite unexpectedly,
The world begins to change,
And I sense something different,
Special and new and strange.

The twins have settled down to read,
My sister's at the shops,
My Dad switches the telly off,
The baby's crying stops,

The dog's asleep, and for some while
The washing hasn't stirred
    – And something enters into my head
    – I've hardly ever heard:

The sound of silence – like a sea
Without the sound of waves,
    – Like mountain tops without the wind,
    – Like subterranean caves

Without the echoes – like a sleep
Nothing on earth can break,
Of soldiers in their graves – except
*I'm* living and awake!

*Alan Brownjohn*

Saturday was named after the Roman god of agriculture, Saturn.

2.   Talk about.

What is your best day of the week? Talk about activities you could do at the weekends to prevent you from getting bored.

3.   Answer the questions.

   a.   How does the sister annoy the parents? _____

   b.   Which of the noises do you think the brothers might make? _____
        _____

   c.   Name two household items that are making a noise.
        _____

   d.   How does the world suddenly change? _____
        _____

   e.   Name one thing to which the poet compares the silence. _____

   f.   How do you think the poet feels about the silence? _____
        _____

4.   Quote from the poem to support the following statements.
     Full sentences are not necessary. Do not forget quotation marks.

   a.   The brothers are joyful children.
        _____

   b.   The dog eats all its food.
        _____

   c.   The washing machine is not new.
        _____

   d.   Dad likes cereal.
        _____

   e.   There are adverts on the TV.
        _____

   f.   Silence is not something the poet often experiences.
        _____

5.   Answer the questions in your copybook.

   a.   How many people are in this family?
   b.   Which of the noises in the poem would irritate you most?
   c.   What noises do you have in your home on a Saturday morning?
   d.   Do you prefer noise or silence? Give a reason for your answer.
   e.   Complete the sentence: Silence is like ...

A simile compares something which is similar or alike in some way. The word **as** or the word **like** is always used in a simile.

> **Sample** The boy was **as mad as a March hare**.

6.  Complete the similes.

| snail | eel | rain | grass | owl | pancake | feather | mule | bee | peacock | ox |
| lamb | fiddle | crystal | ice | coal | honey | snow | church mouse | cucumber |

a.   as wise as an         _____
b.   as sweet as           _____
c.   as stubborn as a      _____
d.   as strong as an       _____
e.   as black as           _____
f.   as busy as a          _____
g.   as slippery as an     _____
h.   as gentle as a        _____
i.   as poor as a          _____
j.   as green as           _____

k.   as fit as a           _____
l.   as light as a         _____
m.   as cool as a          _____
n.   as proud as a         _____
o.   as right as           _____
p.   as slow as a          _____
q.   as cold as            _____
r.   as white as           _____
s.   as clear as           _____
t.   as flat as a          _____

7.  Complete the sentences using suitable similes.

a.   She was _____ preparing for the party.
b.   I felt _____ when I came first in the race.
c.   My brother is _____ and he won't change his mind.
d.   He exercises daily and he is _____.
e.   My teacher knows everything. She is _____.
f.   The kitten only weighs 500g. It is _____.
g.   Your dirty face is _____.
h.   My friend is _____ and it takes him ages to walk to school.
i.   She could not afford to buy any clothes as she was _____.
j.   This delicious milk is _____.

> I'm as bright as a button!

8.  Make up similes of your own.

a.   as good as        _____
b.   as lazy as        _____
c.   as silly as       _____
d.   as tasty as       _____
e.   as wonderful as   _____
f.   as large as       _____
g.   as hungry as      _____
h.   as bright as      _____

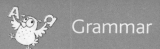

**Remember:** Apostrophes identify the owner of something.

> **Sample** the teacher's cake

If a word already ends in an **s** then you need to an apostrophe and another **s**.

> **Sample** Lewis's poodle

If the word ends in **s** because it is a plural, then put an apostrophe after the **s**.

> **Sample** the ladies' handbags

If the plural does not end in **s** then you need to add an apostrophe and an **s**.

> **Sample** the men's bikes

9. Write these phrases using apostrophes to show the owner.
   a. the hen belonging to Ross _____
   b. the wands belonging to the fairies _____
   c. the crumbs belonging to the mice _____
   d. the TV belonging to John _____
   e. the leaves belonging to the trees _____
   f. the work belonging to the class _____
   g. the false teeth belonging to the men _____
   h. the bowls belonging to the cats _____
   i. the parrot belonging to James _____
   j. the sweets belonging to the children _____

10. Add apostrophes. Rewrite the sentences in your copybook.
    a. Everyone wanted to play Grahams new computer game.
    b. Harrys work was not finished but he did not want Samanthas help.
    c. The fishermens nets were full of fish.
    d. Johns party was good and the magicians tricks were amazing.
    e. The birds nests looked warm and cosy.
    f. The baboons teeth are longer than the lions teeth.
    g. The boys faces were covered in chocolate sauce.
    h. The babies bottles were warmed in hot water.
    i. The thieves masks were left at the scene of the crime.
    j. Jacks father and Darrens uncle are training to run in the marathon.

11. Add capital letters, apostrophes, full stops and commas to these sentences. Rewrite them correctly in your copybook.
    a. the african elephants tusks broke the branches of the tree right off
    b. this hallowe'en i think gregs costume will win first prize
    c. jamies biscuits contained flour butter sugar eggs milk cocoa and baking powder
    d. even though miss berry was willing to take us on an outing she would not take us to dublins best shops
    e. the womens conversations were all about cooking cleaning washing sweeping and looking after children

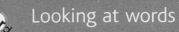

**Word list**

| machine | spills | different | enters | silence |
|---------|--------|-----------|--------|---------|
| mountain | echoes | soldiers | neighbours | sense |

12. Learn the spellings. Now look and say, picture, cover, write, check.

_____     _____

_____     _____

_____     _____

_____     _____

13. Write any words you got wrong.

_____

14. Fill in the missing words. Use the word list.

   a.   Everest is a _____ I'd like to climb.

   b.   The _____ marched in the parade.

   c.   My brother often _____ his juice on the carpet.

   d.   Dogs have a very good _____ of smell.

   e.   The actor _____ onto the stage with a bow.

> My **neighbours** are quite nosy!

15. In your copybook write your own sentences using these words:
    **different**, **silence**, **echoes**, **neighbours** and **machine**.

16. Write the answers. Use the word list.

   a.   Which word from the list has **soft c**? _____

   b.   Find list words that contain these smaller words:

        **chin** _____     **if** _____

        **old** _____     **ours** _____

   c.   Write a list word with a **ch** that sounds like a **k**. _____

   d.   Write a list word with a **ch** that sounds like a **sh**. _____

   e.   Break these words into syllables. Write the number of syllables for each.

        **different** _____     **soldiers** _____

        **spills** _____     **echoes** _____

   f.   Write a word that is in plural form. _____

   g.   Write the last five list words in alphabetical order.

        _____  _____  _____

        _____  _____

   h.   Write a word that has a **silent e**. _____

## Talk about

17. Work with a group to read the poem *Saturday morning where I live*. Discuss the poem and say what you thought of it.

## Write about

18. Create a short song or rhyme using the days of the week.

_____

_____

_____

_____

_____

_____

_____

_____

19. Underline the key words in these sentences.

    Key words are the most important words.

    > **Sample** The brave, little, old **lady hit** the nasty **burglar** over the head with her big, black **umbrella**.

    a. The double-decker tourist bus took all the excited travellers past Dublin's most famous and interesting attractions.

    b. My room is quite tidy, besides the clothes lying on the floor, the half-eaten sandwiches and the pile of papers on the carpet.

20. In your copybook write key words about your Saturday morning.

21. In your copybook write about your Saturday morning using your key words to help you. Read it to a friend.

22. Find ten Saturday activities hiding in these sentences. The first one is already done.

    a. The cat lies on the **rug by** the fire.          **rugby**

    b. Nancy cleans her room daily.          _____

    c. Finches sing beautifully.          _____

    d. Kittens are adorable.          _____

    e. The bin goes outside.          _____

    f. In my home, work is of great importance.          _____

    g. Roisin gets chips on Fridays.          _____

    h. Always wash your underwear.          _____

    i. Treacle and toffee are sweet.          _____

    j. I will kiss Kate under the mistletoe.          _____

 What do you know about Nessie?

1.  Read the newspaper report about the Loch Ness Monster.

# FACT OR FICTION?

### By James Ness

The day, January 31st, 1932, started off as a normal day in the classroom for a group of Scottish children. They had just completed a Maths lesson and were getting ready for break.

During break time, the children played tag in the school grounds. Some children were looking out at the lake in front of their school.

Suddenly one of the children screamed. He pointed to the lake, his eyes wide with fear. The other children looked to where he was pointing. They, too, froze in terror.

The children rushed into the classroom, gasping for breath. Some started crying.

The alarmed teacher tried calming them down. The children claimed they had seen a monster in the marshes of Urquhart Bay. They described it as having a long, thin neck and small head. One child pointed to a picture on the wall and said that was what she had seen. It was a picture of a dinosaur – *Elasmosaurus*. Some of the children cried again when they saw the picture.

Could the children have seen the Loch Ness Monster? Or was it just their wild imagination?

Many people have claimed to have seen the Loch Ness Monster, or Nessie, as she is affectionately called. All sightings have occurred in the same loch – Loss Ness in the centre of Scotland. The monster is described as having a long, thin neck with a snake-like head. It has a large, thick body which is about six metres in length. Photographs and video footage have been taken but no-one is certain if they are authentic. Does Nessie exist? It remains an unsolved mystery.

| The water in Loch Ness is very murky so visibility is not good. |
| --- |

2. Talk about.

Do you think Nessie exists? Discuss your opinions with the class.
Listen to and accept the opinions of others.

Look at the webcam of Loch Ness to see if you can spot Nessie!
www.lochness.co.uk/livecam/

3. Answer the questions.

    a.    In which year did this sighting occur? _____

    b.    Where is Loch Ness? _____

    c.    What were the children doing during break time? _____

    _____

    d.    What did the children claim to have seen? _____

    _____

    e.    Who did the children tell? _____

    _____

    f.    How did the children react to the sighting? _____

    _____

4. Write the meanings of these words in context. Use your dictionary.

    a.    completed    _____

    b.    gasping    _____

    c.    alarmed    _____

    d.    imagination    _____

    e.    occurred    _____

    f.    certain    _____

    g.    authentic    _____

    h    mystery    _____

5. Answer the questions in your copybook.

    a.    What do you think the children saw?

    b.    Do you think the teacher believed them? Give a reason for your answer.

    c.    Do you believe Nessie exists? Say why or why not.

6. In your copybook draw Nessie according to the descriptions in the text. Use labels.

**Remember:** A prefix is a group of letters at the beginning of a word that changes its meaning.

| Sample **dis**honest |

The prefix **tele** means **from a long way away.**

| Sample **tele**gram |

The prefix **bi** means **two.**

| Sample **bi**lingual |

*I clean my room **biannually.***

7. Add the prefix **tele** or **bi** to these words.

a. _____ phone          f. _____ cycle
b. _____ plane          g. _____ vision
c. _____ focals         h. _____ scope
d. _____ monthly        i. _____ sales
e. _____ weekly         j. _____ ceps

The prefixes **in**, **im** and **il**, **ir** and **un** give a word the opposite meaning.

Add **in** or **un** for most words.

For words beginning with **p**, **m** add **im**.

For words beginning with **l** add **il**.

For words beginning with **r** add **ir**.

| Sample **in**edible, **un**fit |

| Sample **im**mobile, **im**proper |

| Sample **il**literate |

| Sample **ir**rational |

*This is illegible!*

8. Add **in**, **im**, **ir** or **il** to these words.

a. _____ polite         f. _____ mature
b. _____ regular        g. _____ legible
c. _____ logical        h. _____ patient
d. _____ complete       i. _____ visible
e. _____ legal          j. _____ literate

The prefix **a** means **on** or **in.**          The prefix **al** means **all.**

| Sample **a**ground |          | Sample **al**together |

*It is illegal to always watch the **tele**vision.*

9. Add **a** or **al** to these words.

a. _____ ways           f. _____ way
b. _____ round          g. _____ most
c. _____ part           h. _____ ready
d. _____ though         i. _____ blaze
e. _____ head           j. _____ one

10. Write 10 silly sentences in your copybook, using words with prefixes.

**Remember:** Speech marks show that someone is speaking.
They go around the actual words people are saying.

| Sample | 'I don't feel like working now,' said Barry.
'Oh, I do!' said Tammy. |

11. Add speech marks and commas. Rewrite the sentences in your copybook.

a. These coffee biscuits taste funny said Rosie.
b. Emma whispered My answer for number five is twenty-one.
c. The toaster is not working grumbled Helena.
d. Please let us play in the snow begged Sandra.
e. Robin said My budgie ate my homework.
f. I do not like shopping for groceries cried Sophie.
g. Break is over now explained the principal.
h. It is too cold to play outside complained Robin.
i. I do not feel like cleaning my room muttered Ed.
j. The forest is on fire shouted Pat.

12. Using speech marks, write what the people are saying. Make up the peoples' names.

a. Please help me!
b. I am feeling rather hungry.
c. I hope Shane loves me too.
d. Did you eat all your vegetables?

a. _____
b. _____
c. _____
d. _____

13. Complete the sentences.

a. '_____,' sobbed Jemma to the teacher.
b. The boy shouted, '_____!'
c. The boy who sits next to me whispered, '_____.'
d. '_____?' asked the principal.
e. The child begged, '_____.'
f. '_____,' said my brother happily.

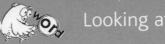
**Word list**

| normal | terror | gasping | calming | claimed |
|--------|--------|---------|---------|---------|
| dinosaur | sightings | metres | length | photographs |

14. Learn the spellings. Now look and say, picture, cover, write, check.

_____     _____

_____     _____

_____     _____

_____     _____

15. Write any words you got wrong.

_____

16. Fill in the missing words. Use the word list.

   a. The child _____ there was a UFO in the back garden.

   b. In a square the _____ and the width are the same.

   c. He was _____ for breath after chasing the thief.

   d. I felt sheer _____ when I saw the spider.

   e. Elasmosaurus is a type of _____.

   > That is not **normal** behaviour.

17 In your copybook write your own sentences using these words:
   **normal**, **calming**, **sightings**, **metres** and **photographs**.

18. Write the answers. Use the word list.

   a. Which words contain these smaller words?

   **error** _____     **aimed** _____

   **calm** _____     **met** _____

   b. Which two words in plural form? _____  _____

   c. Write a word that contains four vowels. _____

   d. Break these words into syllables. Write the number of syllables.

   **dinosaur** _____     **photographs** _____     **normal** _____

   e. Underline the silent letters in **calming** and **sightings**.

   f. Underline the letter pattern that is the same in these words.

   **calming**     **sightings**     **gasping**

   g. Write the root words of these words.

   **sightings** _____     **claimed** _____     **gasping** _____

   h. Take two letters away from each to make words from the list.

   **lengthen** _____     **abnormal** _____

   **exclaimed** _____     **normally** _____

## Talk about

19. Work in pairs. One person says they have seen Nessie and the other plays a reporter. The reporter must ask relevant questions and the witness can make up the details.

## Write about

20. In your copybook write an acrostic poem about Loch Ness. Each word or phrase must begin with the letters of the words. Do your rough work below.

L – _____
O – _____
C – _____
H – _____

N – _____
E – _____
S – _____
S – _____

**Sample**
N – Not a fairytale
E – Eats people that do not believe
S – Swims in the depths
S – Sightings are rare
I – In Loch Ness for centuries
E – Escape if you can

**Remember!**
Loch Ness is the lake.

Check your work. Correct any mistakes, then rewrite or type it out. Display your poems in the classroom.

At its deepest, Loch Ness is 248m deep.

21. Find the monsters in the wordsearch.

| M | e | d | u | s | a | M | o | t | h | r | a | C | u |
| q | w | d | r | t | y | Y | o | m | i | z | a | h | s |
| g | G | r | e | n | d | e | l | f | d | s | a | i | w |
| p | H | a | R | G | o | t | i | u | d | v | y | m | t |
| C | y | c | l | o | p | s | f | K | r | a | k | e | N |
| z | d | u | x | d | c | c | v | G | a | m | e | r | a |
| b | r | l | n | z | m | l | k | o | g | p | Y | a | g |
| h | a | a | g | i | a | n | t | l | o | i | e | d | a |
| s | a | q | w | l | r | t | y | e | n | r | t | i | o |
| t | r | o | l | l | p | o | i | m | u | e | i | t | r |
| e | w | q | a | a | g | r | i | f | f | o | n | f | d |

| Dracula | Medusa | dragon | Hydra | Roc | giant | Kraken | troll | griffon | Grendel |
| vampire | Yeti | Cyclops | Godzilla | Yomi | Naga | Chimera | Golem | Gamera |

Which cities have you been to? Do you live in one?

1. Read the table.

## Table of cities

| City | Country | Natural features | Population | Nickname | Av. Temp – June | Tourist attraction |
|------|---------|------------------|-----------|----------|-----------------|--------------------|
| Paris | France | River Seine | 2.2 million | The City of Lights | 12-21 degrees Celsius | Eiffel Tower |
| Amsterdam | Netherlands | IJ Bay Amstel River | 743,905 | Gateway to Europe | 12-22 | Anne Frank House, canals |
| New York | U.S.A. | Hudson River | 18.7 million | The Big Apple | 17-27 | Statue of Liberty, Times Square |
| Beijing | China | Chaobai River | 8.5 million | The Forbidden City | 19-30 | Great Wall of China |
| Sydney | Australia | Sydney Harbour | 4.2 million | The Harbour City | 9-16 | Opera House |
| Cape Town | South Africa | Table Mountain | 2.9 million | The Mother City | 8-18 | Whale watching |
| Calcutta | India | Ganges Delta | 5 million | City of Palaces | 26-33 | Howrah Bridge |
| Rome | Italy | Tiber River Aniene River | 2.5 million | The Eternal City | 17-33 | Colosseum |
| Rio de Janiero | Brazil | Guanabara Bay | 11-12 million | The Marvellous City | 15-30 | Large annual carnival |
| Moscow | Russia | Moskva River | 10.4 million | The Spirit of Russia | 10-20 | Red Square, Kremlin |
| Galway | Ireland | River Corrib | 71,983 | The City of the Tribes | 8-17 | Irish language, music and dance |

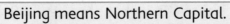
Beijing means Northern Capital.

2.  Talk about.

    Which phrases do we use that might
    not be understood by people from other
    cities or countries?

3.  Answer the questions in your copybook.
    a.   Where is the city of Calcutta?
    b.   Which city has the largest population?
    c.   What is Moscow's nickname?
    d.   Which natural feature can be found in Cape Town?
    e.   Name a city in Australia.
    f.   Where would you find Anne Frank's house?
    g.   Which city has a higher population, Moscow or Beijing?
    h.   Which are the hottest and coldest cities?

4.  Tick the true sentences. Write them in your copybook.
    a.   Beijing has a population of 5 million.
    b.   Paris is known as the Gateway to Europe.
    c.   The River Corrib flows through Galway city.
    d.   The temperature in June in Rome averages between 17 and 33 degrees Celsius.
    e.   Red Square can be found in Calcutta.
    f.   Galway's population is less than 100,000.
    g.   The Chaobai River flows through New York city.
    h.   In Rio de Janeiro the temperature is below 10 degrees in June.
    i.   The Statue of Liberty can be found in Paris, France.
    j.   You can see the Colosseum in Rome, Italy.

5.  Choose one city from the table to write about. Write in full sentences.

    _____
    _____
    _____
    _____
    _____

6.  Answer the questions in your copybook.
    a.   Which city on the table would you like to visit? Give a reason for your answer.
    b.   Which cities have you visited?
    c.   Which city did you like the best? Give a reason for your answer.
    d.   What do you think is the best and worst thing about living in a busy city?

**Remember:** A suffix is a group of letters at the end of a word.

| Sample | thank – thank**ful** |

If a word ends in **e** drop the **e** before adding **ing**.

| Sample | make – making |

Sometimes you need to double the last letter before adding the suffix.

| Sample | sip – sipping |

This laziness will not do!

7. Add the suffix **ing**.

   a.  glide _____      f.  sip _____
   b.  walk _____       g.  freeze _____
   c.  believe _____    h.  prove _____
   d.  shower _____     i.  rewrite _____
   e.  unzip _____      j.  inflate _____

8. Write your own sentence using **ing** words.

   _____

9. Add the suffix **able** or **ness**. (Change **y** to **i** before adding **ness**.)

   a.  kind _____       f.  adjust _____
   b.  happy _____      g.  enjoy _____
   c.  sweet _____      h.  tidy _____
   d.  break _____      i.  afford _____
   e.  sad _____        j.  spread _____

10  Write your own sentence using a **ness** and **able** word.

   _____

11. Add the suffixes **less** and **ful**.

   a.  hope _____       _____
   b.  meaning _____    _____
   c.  pain _____       _____
   d.  colour _____     _____
   e.  power _____      _____
   f.  care _____       _____
   g.  use _____        _____
   h.  taste _____      _____
   i.  thought _____    _____
   j.  harm _____       _____

12. Write your own sentence using a **ful** and **less** word.

   _____

Nouns are naming words.
Common nouns are the names of things.

> **Sample** child, tree, book, shirt

Proper nouns are the names of people, pets, places, dates and titles.

> **Sample** Peter, Ireland, Shannon River, The Himalayas

13. Underline the nouns.

What do you think the <u>moon</u> smells like? It smells a bit like <u>gunpowder</u> apparently. Only twelve <u>people</u> have <u>walked</u> on the <u>moon</u> and they all came from <u>America</u>. Because the astronauts wore airtight space suits, they could not smell anything while on the moon, but the moon dust clung to their suits.

They reported that the moon dust felt like snow, smelled like gunpowder and did not taste too bad.

The idea that the moon was made of cheese dates back to the 16<sup>th</sup> century. A man called John Heywood said in a proverb, 'the moon is made of green cheese'.

> **Remember** Proper nouns begin with a capital letter.

14. Underline the common nouns in red and the proper nouns in blue.
Rewrite the sentences in your copybook, changing the nouns.

   a. My puppy, Bubbles, loves to have a warm and soapy bath.
   b. Dr. Doolittle had a way of talking to the animals.
   c. The class is going to the Gaiety Theatre in Dublin to see a play.
   d. My neighbour, Joan Reilly, is going to Spain for the summer.
   e. Sarah is sitting exams in May and June of this year.
   f. The Spire is located in O'Connell Street in Dublin.
   g. Paul McCartney was a member of the band The Beatles.
   h. Mr. and Mrs. Boyle are visiting the Eiffel Tower in Paris, France.
   i. To celebrate St. Patrick's Day, we are going to have dinner at the Chili Café.
   j. Miss. Brady gives us an English test every Friday.

15. Complete the sentences using suitable nouns. Be creative! Then compare your sentences.

   a. There was a small _____ in our _____ .
   b. I was sitting reading a _____ when the _____ went off.
   c. She was eating a _____ in the _____ .
   d. The _____ fell off the _____ .
   e. The excited _____ were playing in the _____ .
   f. The _____ gave me a _____ .
   g. We sat in the busy _____ and waited for a _____ .
   h. Our _____ broke down so we called a _____ .

**Word list**

| spirit | tourist | harbour | palaces | language | carnival |
| marvellous | France | Amsterdam | Australia | Russia | Italy |

16. Learn the spellings. Now look and say, picture, cover, write, check.

_____     _____
_____     _____
_____  ,  _____
_____     _____
_____     _____
_____     _____

17. Write any words you got wrong.

_____

18. Fill in the missing words. Use the word list.
   a.  Someone who is a traveller or sightseer is a _____.
   b.  We went to the _____ to see the ship coming in.
   c.  The king had a few _____ around the world.
   d.  _____ is known as 'the land down under'.
   e.  The country of _____ is shaped like a boot.
   f.  In _____ the people speak French.

*Carnivals make me sick.*

19. In your copybook write your own sentences using these words:
   **spirit**, **language**, **carnival**, **marvellous**, **Amsterdam** and **Russia**.

20 Write the answers. Use the word list.
   a.  Write the words that have double letters. _____
   b.  Which words contain these smaller words? **our** _____
       **us** _____ **age** _____ **laces** _____
       **ran** _____
   c.  Write a mnemonic that helps you to spell **language**.
       _____
   d.  Write two proper nouns from the list. _____ _____
   e.  Underline the letter pattern that is the same in **tourist** and **harbour**.
   f.  Write a word from the list that has a **soft c**. _____
   g.  Break these words into syllables. Write the number of syllables for each.
       **Amsterdam** ____ **Italy** ____ **marvellous** ____ **language** ____
   h.  Write the last six words from the list in alphabetical order.
       _____     _____
       _____     _____

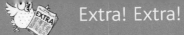

## Talk about

21. Work in pairs. Act out a scene where a tourist must ask a local person for directions to a particular place in the area. The tourist will not speak English very well. The local person must give directions in a simple way, using hand gestures, because the tourist will not understand much English.

## Write about

22. Choose one city in the world you would like to visit. Research the city and in your copybook write some facts about it.

> **Think about:**
> a. Where is the city?
> b. What natural features does it have?
> c. What is the weather like?
> d. What tourist attractions does it have?
> e. What language(s) is/are spoken?
> f. What is the population?
> g. What is interesting about this city?

> Rio de Janeiro means River of January.

> Look at www.wikipedia.org

23. Write out your information neatly. Present it to the class or a group. Also, give your reasons for wanting to visit this city.

24. Write the city names in the grid.

|  |  |  |  | C |  |  |  |  |
|---|---|---|---|---|---|---|---|---|
|  |  |  |  |  |  |  |  |  |
|  |  |  |  |  |  |  |  |  |
|  |  |  | i |  |  |  |  |  |
|  |  |  |  |  |  |  |  |  |
|  |  |  |  |  |  |  |  |  |
|  |  |  |  |  |  |  |  |  |
|  |  | P |  |  |  |  |  |  |
|  |  |  |  |  |  |  |  |  |
|  |  | R |  |  |  |  |  |  |
|  |  |  |  |  |  |  |  |  |
|  |  |  |  |  | a |  |  |  |
|  |  |  |  |  |  |  |  |  |

> Calcutta
> Cairo
> Oslo
> Paris
> Boston
> Mexico (city)
> Beijing
> Geneva
> Rio
> Reno

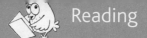
 Before you read...

Can you make any meals on your own?

> **Remember** If you are cooking, there must be an adult present.

1. Read the recipe.

## Chicken curry

Preparation time: less than 30 mins.
Cooking time: 10 to 30 mins.

**Ingredients for the chicken curry:**

1 tbsp oil
1 chicken thigh, chopped into three pieces
onion, diced
1 garlic clove, crushed
1 tsp cayenne pepper
1 tsp curry powder
1 tsp red chilli, diced
150ml chicken stock

**To serve:**
1 tbsp Greek yoghurt

**Ingredients for the rice:**

Onion, diced
1 tbsp oil
1 cup rice
1 tsp curry powder
1 tsp turmeric powder
half a cup of chicken stock
red chilli, diced
a handful of mange tout
2 tbsp butter

> tbsp = tablespoon
> tsp = teaspoon

## Method:

1. For the chicken curry, heat the oil in a deep frying pan. Add the chicken, onion and garlic and cook over a low heat for five minutes to colour the chicken and soften the onion.

2. Add the spices and chilli and stir for one minute.

3. Add the chicken stock and season, to taste, with salt and black pepper. Bring to the boil, then reduce the heat and simmer gently for 15 minutes.

4. Meanwhile, for the rice, heat the oil in a pan. Add the onion and cook for five minutes, until soft.

5. Add the remaining ingredients and bring to the boil. Reduce to a simmer, cover and cook for 15 minutes, or until the rice is cooked.

6. Add the butter to the cooked rice and stir through.

7. To serve, place the rice in a dish, spoon over the curry and top with Greek yoghurt.

2.  Talk about.

    What is your favourite meal? Talk about simple meals
    you could make on your own.

    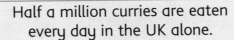

    > Half a million curries are eaten
    > every day in the UK alone.

3.  Answer the questions.

    a.  Which ingredients are cooked first?

    _____

    b.  When is the butter added to the rice?

    _____

    c.  How much chicken stock is needed for the curry and rice?

    _____

    d.  Which ingredients are chopped?

    _____

    e.  What is served with the completed dish?

    _____

    f.  Do you think this meal would be easy to make? Explain your answer.

    _____

4.  Write the meanings of these words. Use your dictionary.

    a.  diced          _____
    b.  stock          _____
    c.  mange tout     _____
    d.  reduce         _____
    e.  simmer         _____
    f.  season to taste _____

5.  In your copybook write these sentences in order to cook the chicken.

    a.  Add spices and chilli.
    b.  Bring it to the boil.
    c.  Season to taste.
    d.  Fry the chicken, onion and garlic.
    e.  Reduce the heat and simmer.
    f.  Add the chicken stock.

6.  Answer the questions in your copybook.

    a.  Would you like to eat this chicken curry? Give a reason for your answer.
    b.  What is your favourite meal?
    c.  Write five important rules for keeping safe in the kitchen.

7.  Underline the prefixes. Write the **root** words.

> Sample  un**accept**able.  The root word is **accept**.

a.   telegraph _____
b.   impossible _____
c.   incorrect _____
d.   aloud _____
e.   bicycle _____
f.   impatient _____

g.   inaccurate _____
h.   illegal _____
i.   irresponsible _____
j.   imperfect _____
k.   already _____
l.   disadvantage _____

8.  Write your own sentence using words with **prefixes**.

_____

9.  Underline the suffixes. Write the **root** words.

a.   fixable _____
b.   breathing _____
c.   printable _____
d.   breakable _____
e.   tearful _____
f.   travelling _____

g.   heartless _____
h.   wonderful _____
i.   thoughtless _____
j.   whipping _____
k.   tiring _____
l.   comfortable _____

10.  Write your own sentence using some words with **suffixes**.

_____

11.  Underline the **prefixes** and **suffixes**. Write the root words.

a.   illegally _____
b.   unreliable _____
c.   inflexible _____
d.   impoliteness _____
e.   unthankful _____
f.   impatiently _____
g.   disappearance _____
h.   misunderstanding _____
i.   inconsiderate _____
j.   unappealing _____

Please stop being so careless!

12.  In your copybook write prefixes and/or suffixes to these words. Try to add both.

a.   friend     c.   love     e.   trust     g.   write     i.   treat
b.   secure     d.   cover     f.   please     h.   correct     j.   charge

Verbs are action words.

> **Sample** He **watches** too much TV. He **is** quite lazy.

13. Underline the verbs.

Do you know which African animal is the most dangerous? It is the hippopotamus. The hippo belongs to the pig family and there are two species: Common and Pygmy. Not many animals are stupid enough to attack a hippo. Do not be fooled by its bulky size because it can run very fast – faster than you. It is a vegetarian and eats mainly grass. The skin of a hippo weighs a ton and is 4 centimetres thick. A hippo is adapted to spending time in the water and it can close its nostrils and stay under water for up to five minutes. A hippo has four teeth, made of ivory. People say that it has very bad breath.

14. Complete the sentences using suitable verbs. Make sure you use the same tense in each sentence.

a. The soldiers _____ across the field and _____ their guns.

b. The boy _____ on the chair and _____ .

c. The chef _____ the meal but the customers do not _____ it.

d. The baby _____ all morning and _____ all night.

e. My family _____ outside to watch the hedgehogs _____ .

f. The teacher _____ when she sees the mouse _____ away.

g. The policeman _____ the thief who tries to _____ .

h. This class _____ during class time and they _____ during break time.

Some verbs aren't just single words. They need a helping verb as well.

> **Sample** It **was** raining. **Was** is a helping verb.

15. Add the right helping verbs. Rewrite the sentences in your copybooks. Some sentences have more than one possible answer.

> could    have    is    does    be    might    will    was    are    has

a. The spaceship _____ arrived to take you home.

b. My Dad _____ driving to Donegal.

c. I _might_ visit my teacher on Saturday.

d. We _are_ hoping to have no homework.

e. The class _____ talk quietly.

f. The teacher _____ give us a treat if we behave.

g. The birds _____ built their nests.

h. The mouse _____ peeking out of the hole.

i. Dad must _____ sleeping in his chair by the fire.

j. The dog _____ catch the ball if you throw it correctly.

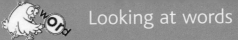
## Word list

| | | | | | | |
|---|---|---|---|---|---|---|
| onion | pepper | crushed | slightly | yoghurt | soften | |
| reduce | teaspoon | ingredients | recipe | season | meanwhile | |

16. Learn the spellings. Now look and say, picture, cover, write, check.

_____   _____
_____   _____
_____   _____
_____   _____
_____   _____

17. Write any words you got wrong.

_____

18. Fill in the missing words. Use the word list.

a. _____ is a dairy product.

b. Adding too much _____ will make your meal hot.

c. Peeling an _____ can sometimes make you cry.

d. Always use a _____ when you bake a cake.

e. The weather is _____ better today.

f. To help save our environment, the motto is:
_____, reuse and recycle.

> There must be something wrong with the **recipe**!

19. In your copybook write your own sentences using these words:
**crushed**, **soften**, **ingredients**, **season**, **meanwhile** and **teaspoon**.

20 Answer the questions.

a. Underline the silent letters in **yoghurt** and **soften**.

b. Write two words from the list that have a **soft c**. _____

c. Find smaller words in these words: **onion** _____
**slightly** _____ **yoghurt** _____ **season** _____

d. Break these words into syllables. Write the number of syllables for each.
**meanwhile** _____ **ingredients** _____ **onion** _____

e. Write the words that rhyme with **nightly** _____ and
**coffin** _____

f. Write a noun from the word list. _____

g. Write the root words of these words:
**soften** _____ **slightly** _____ **crushed** _____

h. Break these words into two smaller words:
**meanwhile** = _____ + _____
**teaspoon** = _____ + _____

**Talk about**

21. Work in a group. Decide what you could make with the following ingredients:

    A piece of chicken, a tomato, an onion, a potato, a carrot, a cup of rice and some cooking oil.

22. Act out a cooking programme, like *Ready, Steady, Cook*, and explain what you are doing with your ingredients.

**Write about**

23. Write a recipe. Include a list of ingredients and the method. Do your rough work below.

| RECIPE | |
|---|---|
| **Ingredients** | **Method** |
| | |

24  Type your recipe neatly and add an illustration. Put all the recipes together in a class booklet and display it in the classroom.

25. Some of the words in this recipe have wrong letters. Change one letter in the underlined words so that the recipe makes sense. Rewrite it in your copybook.

## *Mixed mushroom omelette*

Ingredients:

1 tbsp olive <u>ail</u>          2 tbsp <u>bitter</u>, chopped
200g mixed mushrooms, <u>spiced</u>   1 <u>close</u> of garlic, finely <u>shopped</u>
<u>Rhyme</u> leaves, chopped      1 tbsp <u>demon</u> juice
Parsley leaves, <u>chipped</u>      3 eggs, <u>tightly</u> beaten
<u>Silt</u> and <u>popper</u> to taste    2 tbsp <u>graded</u> cheese

Method:

1. Heat oil and butter in a <u>crying</u> pan.
2. Add mushrooms and fry for <u>night</u> minutes.
3. Add garlic, thyme, lemon juice, parsley and seasoning. <u>Look</u> for another minute.
4. Cook the egg <u>fixture</u> for five minutes.
5. <u>Plane</u> mushroom mixture onto the omelette and sprinkle with cheese.
6. <u>Hold</u> the omelette in half and cook for another minute.
7. <u>Nerve</u> on a plate.
8. Repeat with the <u>test</u> of the ingredients.

Chicken Tikka Masala is the best selling curry. It was invented in Glasgow.

Where is the closest countryside to you? Maybe you are lucky enough to live in it!

**Before you read...**

1. Read the Countryside Code.

If you live in the countryside, or if you're just going for a visit, there are a few things you need to remember.

- Don't light any fires! Fire destroys woodlands and habitats. It can also kill birds and other wildlife.
- Be aware on country roads and always walk on the right-hand side. In addition to cars, there will also be tractors and farm animals! Don't be alarmed if you come across a flock of sheep in the middle of the road. Just stay calm!
- Don't enter private property unless you have permission to do so. Just because you are in the country does not mean you can wander anywhere.
- If you are out walking, stay on the paths. Do not walk through meadows or crops and stay away from haystacks.
- Close any gates that you open. An open gate allows livestock to stray. This could be dangerous to motorists, the animals and you! Avoid climbing over hedges, fences and walls.
- If you have your pet poodle with you, put it on a lead. Dogs can worry and hurt farm animals and wildlife.
- Don't make too much noise! Loud music and noisy behaviour disturb the peace of the countryside. Listen to birdsong instead of your rock music! Avoid other activities that will disturb wildlife such as stone throwing. The countryside is a calm environment – keep it that way.
- Protect wildlife at all times. Never interfere with birds or wild animals or their nests and homes. Don't damage trees by carving your girlfriend/boyfriend's name on them.
- Always take your litter home. Litter is not only ugly but dangerous to wildlife.

These rules do not mean you can't enjoy yourself in the countryside. Have respect for it and enjoy its slower pace and serenity.

2.  Talk about.

Have a class vote to see how many of you would like to live in the countryside and how many would like to live in the city.

Write the results:

**Countryside** _____  **City** _____

Talk about the advantages and disadvantages of living in the countryside.

3.  Answer the questions.

a.  What damage could a fire cause?

    _____

b.  Why should you walk on the right-hand side?

    _____

c.  What could happen if gates were left open?

    _____

d.  Should you play loud music in the countryside? Explain your answer.

    _____

e.  What should you do with your litter?

    _____

4.  Answer the questions in your copybook.

a.  Name two things, other than cars, that you could encounter on country roads.
b.  If a sign says 'Private Property' what should you do?
c.  Why shouldn't you walk freely across meadows?
d.  Could you take your dog to the countryside? Explain your answer.
e.  What sounds of nature might you hear in the countryside?
f.  Why is it important not to drop litter?
g.  Describe the countryside in your own words.
h.  Write an advantage of living in the countryside.
i.  Write a disadvantage of living in the countryside.
j.  Would you prefer living in the city or in the countryside? Give a reason for your answer.

5.  Find words in the Code with the same meaning. Use your dictionary.

a.  where an animal or plant lives  _____
b.  surprised  _____
c.  go in  _____
d.  walk about  _____
e.  drivers  _____
f.  peaceful  _____
g.  unsightly  _____
h.  rubbish  _____

Some words look and sound similar. They have some letters in common. These are called letter patterns.

> **Sample** **g**ive, **l**ive

Some letter patterns look the same but sound different.

> **Sample** t**ough**, thr**ough**, c**ough**, pl**ough**

6. Match the words that have the same letter patterns.
   Draw a solid line if they sound the same and a dotted line if they sound different.

   a.   tough      put
   b.   match      poor
   c.   but        home
   d.   gnome      spread
   e.   cost       rough
   f.   smart      drown
   g.   share      watch
   h.   plead      post
   i.   known      start
   j.   floor      scare

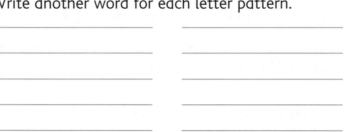

Write another word for each letter pattern.

_____     _____

_____     _____

_____     _____

_____     _____

We'll **soon** be on the m**oon**.

7. Underline the letter patterns. Circle the word that sounds different.

   a.   cone, one, bone        f.   bead, head, bread
   b.   pull, dull, gull       g.   nose, lose, rose
   c.   foot, root, boot       h.   rush, bush, push
   d.   crow, blow, now        i.   bought, thought, through
   e.   bear, hear, dear       j.   death, Meath, breath

8. Write at least three words for each letter pattern.
   Do all the words in each line sound the same?

   a.   **ove** as in sh**ove**l      _____
   b.   **our** as in t**our**ist     _____
   c.   **ind** as in bl**ind**       _____
   d.   **eat** as in ch**eat**       _____
   e.   **ood** as in bl**ood**       _____
   f.   **ook** as in br**ook**       _____
   g.   **ey** as in monk**ey**       _____
   h.   **igh** as in sl**igh**t      _____
   i.   **eak** as in bl**eak**       _____
   j.   **oth** as in b**oth**er      _____

> Take note of letter patterns in your reading and spelling.
> They can help you with both!

9. Add speech marks, capital letters, commas, question marks, exclamation marks, apostrophes and full stops. Rewrite the sentences correctly in your copybook.

   a. i think dublin is better than london answered donna

   b. is this your best work the teacher enquired

   c. watch out mr brady is on his way shouted lenny

   d. i couldnt buy the babies nappies at debbies shop said william

   e. can we play chess hangman scrabble and monopoly asked rebecca

   f. the dentist said gently dont worry this wont hurt a bit

   g. you must wear your seatbelt scolded the garda

   h. kevin asked do you really like brussel sprouts

   i. mum shouted at bill find that pet spider immediately

   j. why are you wearing your pyjamas asked the teacher crossly

10. Underline the nouns in red and the verbs in blue.

Do you know where most tigers live? It is in the USA. One hundred years ago, there were about 40,000 tigers in India, but this number has dropped to between 3,000 and 4,700. There are thought to be 4,000 tigers living in captivity in Texas alone. Perhaps as many as 12,000 tigers are being kept privately as pets in America. Mike Tyson, the boxer, owns four of them. Many states have no laws against owing tigers and they are not expensive either. A tiger cub could cost about $1000.

By the 1950s tigers were extinct around the Caspian Sea, and the tigers on the islands of Bali and Java have completely disappeared. The South China tiger is nearly extinct in the wild, with only about 30 remaining.

Tigers do not like the smell of alcohol and will often attack a person who has been drinking alcohol.

11. Add capital letters, full stops, commas and apostrophes. Rewrite the sentences correctly in your copybook.

   a. we go to school on mondays tuesdays wednesdays thursdays and fridays

   b. although rogers homework was not complete the teacher gave him another chance

   c. i would love to go to paris but maggie wants to go to barcelona

   d. st brendan was born near tralee in county kerry

   e. the smallest dog recorded was a yorkshire terrier owned by arthur maples it was 9.5cm from its nose to its tail

   f. mr and mrs fitzpatrick live in college street in cavan but they also have homes in spain italy portugal florida and washington

   g. mount etna in sicily is one of europes most active volcanoes

   h. the childrens lunch packs consisted of fruit yoghurt sandwiches cheese and water

   i. kelly james jason luke and paddy are going to a match in croke park on sunday

   j. i am reading *harry potter* and josie is reading the *irish times*

**Word list**

| | | | | | |
|---|---|---|---|---|---|
| countryside | wildlife | aware | wander | meadows | livestock |
| motorists | avoid | activities | damage | litter | respect |

12. Learn the spellings. Now look and say, picture, cover, write, check.

_____     _____

_____     _____

_____     _____

_____     _____

_____     _____

13. Write any words you got wrong.

_____

14. Fill in the missing words. Use the word list.

> This feels just like the **countryside**.

   a.   The _____ drove carefully in the rain.

   b.   The farmer makes sure his _____ are well fed.

   c.   You should not _____ around at night.

   d.   Always show _____ to your parents.

   e.   We do art _____ on Fridays.

   f.   _____ belongs in a bin.

15. In your copybook write your own sentences using these words:
    **wildlife**, **countryside**, **aware**, **meadows**, **avoid** and **damage**.

> **Remember**  Compound words are made of two words
> **Example**    **sunshine**

16. Answer the questions. Use the word list.

   a.   Write two compound words from the list. _____  _____

   b.   Which words from the list are in plural form?

        _____

   c.   Which words contain these words?
        **it** _____ **and** _____

   d.   Write a word from the list that has a **soft g**. _____

   e.   Write a word that has double letters. _____

   f.   Change one letter in each of these words to form words from the list.
        **award** _____  **wonder** _____  **letter** _____

   g.   Write the last six words from the list in alphabetical order.

        _____

## Talk about

17. Work in a group. Recite the poem *Sunday in the yarm fard*. Can you swap the sounds around so that they make sense?

### Sunday in the yarm fard

The mat keowed
The mow cooed
The bog darked
The kigeon pooed

The squicken chalked
The surds bang
The kwuk dacked
The burch rells chang

And then, after all the dackling and the changing
The chalking and the banging
The darking and the pooing
The keowing and the cooing
There was a mewtiful Beaumont
Of queace and pie-ate.

*Trevor Millum*

## Write about

18. Work in pairs. In your copybook write a ten point code for living in the city. Write your key words here.

19. Write out your City Codes neatly. Put them together as a class booklet for display.

20. How many words can you make from the word **countryside**? The letters can be in any order.

COUNTRYSIDE

What do you think a traditional Christmas dinner consists of?

*Before you read...*

1. Read the poem.

## Talking turkeys

Be nice to yu turkeys dis christmas
Cos turkeys jus wanna hav fun
Turkeys are cool, turkeys are wicked
An every turkey has a Mum.
Be nice to yu turkeys dis christmas,
Don't eat it, keep it alive,
It could be yu mate an not on yu plate
Say, Yo! Turkey I'm on your side.

I got lots of friends who are turkeys
An all of dem fear christmas time,
Dey wanna enjoy it, dey say humans destroyed it
And humans are out of dere mind,
Yeah, I got lots of friends who are turkeys
Dey all have a right to a life,
Not to be caged up an genetically made up
By any farmer an his wife.

Turkeys jus wanna play reggae
Turkeys jus wanna hip-hop
Can yu imagine a nice young turkey saying,
'I cannot wait for de chop'?
Turkeys like getting presents, dey wanna watch Christmas TV,
Turkeys hav brains and turkeys feel pain
In many ways like yu an me.

I once knew a turkey called Turkey.
He said, 'Benji explain to me please,
Who put de turkey in christmas
An what happens to christmas trees?'
I said, 'I am not too sure turkey
But it's nothing to do wid Christ Mass
Humans get greedy an waste more dan need be
An business men mek loadsa cash.'

Be nice to yu turkey dis christmas
Unvite dem indoors fe sum greens
Let dem eat cake an let dem partake
In a plate of organic grown beans,
Be nice to yu turkey dis christmas
An spare dem de cut of de knife,
Join turkeys United an dey'll be delighted
An yu will mek new friends 'FOR LIFE'.

A male turkey is called a rooster, a female turkey is called a hen and a baby turkey is called a poult.

*Benjamin Zephaniah*

2. **Talk about.**

   Say what you think of the poem. Give your own reactions to what the poet is saying. Do you agree with him?

3. **Answer the questions.**

   a.   How does the poet feel about turkeys?

   _____

   b.   According to the poet, how do turkeys feel about Christmas?

   _____

   c.   What name does Turkey call the poet?

   _____

   d.   How might humans be greedy at Christmas time?

   _____

   e.   Name one thing the poet says we should do for turkeys.

   _____

   f.   Give the poem another title.

   _____

> A turkey never voted for an early Christmas.

4. **Complete the sentences. Use formal English.**

   According to the poem:

   a.   The turkeys say humans _____ Christmas.

   b.   Turkeys have a _____ to life.

   c.   They enjoy reggae and _____ music.

   d.   They feel _____ like you and I do.

   e.   The business men make _____ of money.

   f.   A turkey could be a _____ for life.

5. **In your copybook write these sentences in formal English.**

   a.   Turkeys just wanna hav fun.

   b.   Be nice to yu turkeys dis christmas.

   c.   Business men mek loadsa cash.

   d.   Let dem eat cake and let dem partake.

   e.   Invite dem indoors fe sum greens.

6. **Answer the questions in your copybook.**

   a.   What do you think the poet might have for Christmas dinner?

   b.   What do you have for your Christmas dinner?

   c.   What is the most special day of the year for you? Explain why.

An abbreviation is a word that has been shortened.

> **Sample**  **Mr.** is an abbreviation of **Mister**; **e.g.** is an abbreviation of **example**.

An acronym is when the names of companies or organisations have been shortened by using the first letter of each word.

> **Sample**  **University College Galway** is abbreviated to **UCG**.

7.   Match the abbreviations to the full word.

| | | |
|---|---|---|
| a. | Prof. | Cash on delivery |
| b. | USA | Doctor |
| c. | Capt. | Professor |
| d. | COD | General Practitioner |
| e. | RTE | United States of America |
| f. | Dr | University College Cork |
| g. | Ave | World Health Organisation |
| h. | UCC | Captain |
| i. | GP | Radio Teilifís Eireann |
| j. | WHO | Avenue |

> Fetch the PC A.S.A.P. from Fr. Tom in Green Cres.

8.   Write the abbreviations in full.

   a.   St. Patrick _____
   b.   Yellow Brick Rd _____
   c.   Rev. Smith _____
   d.   Co. Louth _____
   e.   EU _____
   f.   RIP _____
   g.   km / h _____
   h.   PTO _____
   i    Mon 10th Dec _____
   j    UK _____

9.   Write the abbreviated forms.

   a.   Gaelic Athletic Association _____
   b.   Father Thomas McKiernan _____
   c.   Very important person _____
   d.   Big Bottles Limited _____
   e.   Green Street _____
   f.   Electricity Supply Board _____
   g.   Tuesday the 14th February _____
   h.   Dublin Area Rapid Transport _____
   i.   Five degrees Centigrade _____
   j.   Republic of Ireland _____

Adjectives are words that describe nouns.

> **Sample** I have a **friendly, yellow** snake.

10. In your copybook rewrite this paragraph adding adjectives to describe the nouns.

> I have a **cat**. It is a **pet**. It has **stripes** on its tail and a **spot** on its cheek. It needs **exercise** and I take it for a **walk**. It likes **meat** and **fish**. Sometimes it brings me a **mouse** as a **gift**.

11. Form adjectives from these words, example **love – lovely**.

| | | | | | |
|---|---|---|---|---|---|
| a. | juice | _____ | k. | reason | _____ |
| b. | silence | _____ | l. | strength | _____ |
| c. | expense | _____ | m. | grace | _____ |
| d. | power | _____ | n. | beauty | _____ |
| e. | snow | _____ | o. | danger | _____ |
| f. | success | _____ | p. | patience | _____ |
| g. | sun | _____ | q. | wood | _____ |
| h. | thought | _____ | r. | sleep | _____ |
| i. | remark | _____ | s. | use | _____ |
| j. | sense | _____ | t. | respect | _____ |

When we compare adjectives, we use the comparative and superlative form of the word.

> **Sample** big – bigger – biggest

Sometimes we use the words **more** and **most**.

> **Sample** beautiful, more beautiful, most beautiful

12. Write the comparative and superlative forms.

| | | | |
|---|---|---|---|
| a. | funny | _____ | _____ |
| b. | expensive | _____ | _____ |
| c. | fine | _____ | _____ |
| d. | exciting | _____ | _____ |
| e. | horrible | _____ | _____ |
| f. | thin | _____ | _____ |
| g. | dangerous | _____ | _____ |
| h. | warm | _____ | _____ |
| i. | heavy | _____ | _____ |
| j. | friendly | _____ | _____ |
| k. | sad | _____ | _____ |
| l. | hard-working | | |

**Word list**

| turkeys | greedy | destroyed | imagine | explain | waste |
|---------|--------|-----------|---------|---------|-------|
| business | partake | organic | spare | grown | Christmas |

13. Learn the spellings. Now look and say, picture, cover, write, check.

_____     _____
_____     _____
_____     _____
_____     _____
_____     _____

14. Write any words you got wrong.

_____

15. Fill in the missing words. Use the word list.

   a.     The whole class should _____ in the school play.

   b.     _____ vegetables are not sprayed with insecticides.

   c.     Can you _____ what it would be like to be invisible?

   d.     Their shed was _____ in a fire.

   e.     Turn off taps so you do not _____ water.

   f.     _____ is celebrated on the 25th December.

*Would you care to explain?*

16. In your copybook write your own sentences using these words:
**turkeys**, **explain**, **business**, **spare**, **grown** and **greedy**.

17. Write the answers. Use the word list.

   a.     Find smaller words in:

          **waste** _____ **grown** _____ **spare** _____

   b.     Write a word from the list with a **soft g**. _____

   c.     Break these words into syllables. Write the number of syllables:

          **imagine** _____ **organic** _____ **business** _____ **greedy** _____

   d.     Write a word that has a **silent e**. _____

   e.     Write the root of these words: **grown** _____

          **destroyed** _____ **turkeys** _____ **greedy** _____

   f.     Change one letter in each word to form words from the list:

          **spark** _____ **taste** _____ **brown** _____

   g.     Write the words from the list that have double letters. _____

          _____

   h.     Write words that rhyme with:

          **chased** _____ **wear** _____ **stone** _____

## Talk about

18. Work in a group. Recite the poem *Talking turkeys*.

## Write about

19. In your copybook write a poem about Christmas, or your special celebration day. Follow the format. You do not have to write full sentences. Be creative and use plenty of descriptive words!

Line 1: Name of holiday

Line 2: Something you see on this holiday

Line 3: Something you smell on this holiday

Line 4: Something you hear on this holiday

Line 5: Something you taste on this holiday

Line 6: Something you touch on this holiday

Line 7: Another name for this holiday

**Example**

*Hallowe'en*

Witches, wizards, weirdos,
Fear hanging in the air,
Children screaming, 'Trick or treat!'
Too many sweets, too many peanuts,
Slime, fake blood, cobwebs.
Fright Night!

20. Get a partner to check your work and correct any mistakes. Rewrite it neatly and display your poems in the school where visitors can read them.

21. Replace the incorrect words in this Christmas menu with rhyming words. Rewrite it in your copybook.

**Starters:**
- Turkey and vegetable stoop
- Melon sliced with noun sugar
- Boot selection

| | | |
|---|---|---|
| plum | sprouts | fruit |
| roast | brown | ham |
| soup | mince | creamed |
| gravy | carrots | brandy |
| slice | pies | bread |

**Main courses:**
- Stuffed ghost turkey
- Baked tram
- Vegetables:
    dreamed potatoes, Brussel doubts,
    parrots and parsnips
- Dread sauce, Navy

Turkeys do not come from Turkey.

**Desserts:**
- Rinse prize with sandy sauce
- Drum pudding
- Mice of Christmas cake

Do you know where India is?

1. Read the story.

## *The drum* – a tale from India

A poor woman had only one son. She worked hard every day, cleaning houses for the richer families in town. In return, these families gave her some grain, but she could never afford to buy nice things for her son.

One day, as she was about to leave for the market to sell some grain, she said to her son, 'What can I get you from the market?'
The son replied, 'I would love to have a drum.'

The mother knew she could not afford to buy a drum. As she returned from the market with the flour and salt she was able to buy, she saw a nice piece of wood on the road. She picked it up and gave it to her son. He did not know what to do with it!

He carried the piece of wood as he went out to play. An old woman was struggling to light her fire and she was in tears.
The boy said, 'I have a nice piece of wood you can start your fire with.' He gave the old woman the piece of wood. She lit the fire and she was very pleased. She made some bread and gave the boy a piece of freshly baked bread.

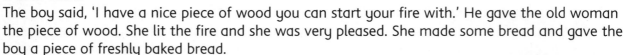

He took the bread and walked on. Soon, he found the potter's wife trying to console a child.
The boy asked, 'Why is the child crying?'
The woman answered, 'The child is hungry and I have nothing to give him.'
The boy quickly gave the piece of bread to the child, who ate it eagerly,and stopped crying. The potter's wife was pleased and gave the boy a pot.

He walked on and came to a river, where he saw a washerman and his wife having an argument. He was shouting that his wife had broken the only laundry pot they had.
The boy said, 'Please don't argue any more. You can have my pot.' They were very pleased and in return, they gave the boy a coat.

He walked on and came across a man who was shivering from the cold. He asked the man, 'Where is your shirt and coat?'
'They have been stolen from me,' said the cold man.
'Don't worry,' said the boy. 'You can have this coat.'
'You are very kind,' answered the man gratefully. 'I will give you this horse.'

The boy took the horse and rode on. Soon he came to a wedding party, with musicians, the bridegroom and his family. They all looked sad.

'What is the matter?' asked the boy.

The bridegroom answered, 'I need a horse to get to the church where I will be married. The man who was supposed to bring a horse has not arrived. I will miss my own wedding!'

The boy said, 'Here, you can take this horse.'

The people were delighted. 'What can I do for you in return?' asked the bridegroom. 'Just name it!'

Pointing to the musicians, the boy said, 'You can give me something – that drum the musician has.'

The bridegroom asked the drummer if the boy could have it and the drummer agreed. He knew he could buy another one.

The boy rushed home to his mother, beating his new drum. He told her the whole story of how he'd managed to get a drum, starting off with just having a piece of wood.

2.   Talk about.

As a class, imagine this story takes place in Ireland. Retell the story, giving it an Irish flavour!

3.   Answer the questions in your copybook.

   a.   What job did the boy's mother have?
   b.   What did she buy from the market?
   c.   Who gave the boy some bread?
   d.   Why was the washerman arguing with his wife?
   e    To whom did the boy give a coat?
   f.   How did the boy help the bridegroom?
   g.   Where did the boy get the drum from?

4.   Quote from the story to prove the following. Write the answers in your copybook.
     Do not forget the quotation marks.

   a.   The boy's mother did not receive money for her job.
   b.   The boy was not sure what the piece of wood was for.
   c.   The woman with no fire was upset.
   d.   The child ate the bread quickly.
   e.   The washerman was raising his voice.
   f.   The drummer was happy to give his drum away.
   g.   The boy hurried to his mother.

5.   In your copybook answer **yes**, **no** or **maybe**. Give a reason for your answer.

   a.   The mother looked for a drum at the market.
   b.   The child who was hungry continued to sob.
   c.   The washerman was washing clothes in the river.
   d.   The bridegroom did not want to give the boy anything.
   e.   The boy told his mother every detail of how he had got the drum.

6.   Answer the questions in your copybook.

   a.   Do you think the boy realised they were poor? Give a reason for you answer.
   b.   What kind of character do you think the boy had?
   c.   What do you think the boy's Mum would have said when he returned with the drum?
   d.   What can we learn from this story?
   e.   Name one thing you would love to have.

# Unit 9  Working with words

Many words come from one original root word.

> Sample **sign** (root word) – **sign**posted, **sign**al, **sign**ed, **sign**ature

Often the root word can help you work out what the new word is.

7. Write the root word for each list.

   a.    drying, dry-cleaning, drip-dry          _____
   b.    reset, setback, setting                 _____
   c.    printer, reprint, printable             _____
   d.    filling, filler, refill                 _____
   e.    displace, placemat, replace             _____
   f.    knowing, knowledge, unknown             _____
   g.    photograph, graphic, geography          _____
   h.    forceful, forced, enforce               _____
   i.    asleep, sleepy, sleepwalker             _____
   j.    mistrust, trustworthy, trusting         _____

> Use your dictionary.

8. Write the root of these words. Write another word that can be formed from the root word.

| | | Root word | Another word |
|---|---|---|---|
| a. | personality | _____ | _____ |
| b. | unhelpful | _____ | _____ |
| c. | sickness | _____ | _____ |
| d. | uneasy | _____ | _____ |
| e. | imprisonment | _____ | _____ |
| f. | dreamily | _____ | _____ |
| g. | reddening | _____ | _____ |
| h. | roundabout | _____ | _____ |
| i. | multimillionaire | _____ | _____ |
| j. | enlighten | _____ | _____ |

9. Add prefixes and/or suffixes to the root words to make new words.

   a.    truth       _____
   b.    out         _____
   c.    take        _____
   d.    pay         _____
   e.    able        _____
   f.    live        _____
   g.    move        _____
   h.    complete    _____
   i.    light       _____
   j.    hurt        _____

> The teacher tells me I must **work**. I am **working**! I **worked** yesterday too. I am a **hard-working** person!

52

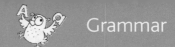

A preposition links nouns, pronouns and phrases to other words in a sentence.

> **Sample** The rabbit ran **under** the fence.

**10.** Use prepositions to complete the sentences. Rewrite the sentences in your copybook.

> with   into   through   behind   between   around   off   since   near   down

a.   Frank looked _____ the window.
b.   They chased each other _____ the playground.
c.   He ran _____ the road.
d.   The chickens walked _____ the farmhouse.
e.   The old man lived _____ the mountain.
f.   Place some ham _____ the slices of bread.
g.   It is scary to jump _____ the diving board.
h.   I am going to a concert _____ my parents.
i.   The class has not stopped working _____ break time.
j.   I know the dog is hiding _____ the door.

> There is more than one possibility.

**11.** Add prepositions to make full sentences. Rewrite the sentences in your copybook.

> about   over   by   from   beside   under   across   until   in   into

a.   Leona crawled her bed.
b.   I park my bike the tree.
c.   Kevin jumped the puddle.
d.   Jane went the bridge.
e.   Arthur sat Ciara and Julie.
f.   I won't do my homework my TV programme is finished.
g.   We are learning bugs in Science.
h.   It costs €5 to go the museum.
i.   Can you jump the fence?
j.   We got gifts our grandparents.

> I jumped **on** my bed, I jumped **off** my bed and then I jumped **into** bed.

**12.** Use these phrases to write sentences of your own.

a.   went with   _____
b.   agreed to   _____
c.   different from   _____
d.   wrote to   _____
e.   blamed for   _____
f.   ashamed of   _____
g.   rely on   _____
h.   inspired by   _____

**Word list**

| returned | afford | struggling | market | eagerly | argument | managed |
|----------|--------|------------|--------|---------|----------|---------|
| laundry | shivering | answered | church | supposed | bridegroom | gratefully |

13.　Learn the spellings. Now look and say, picture, cover, write, check.

_____　　　_____

_____　　　_____

_____　　　_____

_____　　　_____

_____　　　_____

_____　　　_____

14.　Write any words you got wrong.

_____

15.　Fill in the missing words. Use the word list.

　　a.　Have you _____ your library books yet?

　　b.　Throw your muddy clothes in the _____ basket.

　　c.　The _____ bells will ring at midday.

　　d.　We are _____ waiting for the mid-term break.

　　e.　Are you sure you can _____ that diamond ring?

　　f.　The bride and _____ sat in the limousine.

16.　In your copybook write your own sentences using these words:

　　**market**, **struggling**, **argument**, **shivering**, **answered**,
　　**supposed**, **managed** and **gratefully**.

> Oops, I was **supposed** to turn off the oven.

17.　Write the answers. Use the word list.

　　a.　Write the words from the list that have double letters.

　　　_____

　　　_____

　　b.　What is the root of each of these words?

　　　**returned** _____　**struggling** _____

　　　**argument** _____　**managed** _____

　　　**eagerly** _____　**gratefully** _____

　　c.　Which word from the list has a **silent w?** _____

　　d.　Underline the suffixes in these words: **gratefully　eagerly　answered**

　　e.　Break these words into syllables. Write the number of syllables for each.

　　　**struggling** _____　**argument** _____　**shivering** _____　**church** _____

　　f.　Which word starts and ends with the same sound? _____

　　g.　Write a noun from the word list. _____

## Talk about

18. Work with a group. Act out the story of *The drum*.
Some members may have to play two roles. There should be
roles for the boy, his mother and all people he encounters.

## Write about

19. It is important to write a plan before writing a story.

> Tips on how to plan your story:
> ● Decide where your story is going to take place (the setting).
> ● Decide what is going to happen (the plot).
> ● Decide who will be in your story (the characters).
> ● Decide on the beginning, the middle and the end of the story.

In your copybook write a plan for a story called *The Irish boy who wanted a guitar*.
You can use these headings for your plan: Setting / Plot / Characters / Beginning of
the story / Middle of the story / Ending

The Taj Mahal is a famous mausoleum in India.

20. Use your plan and write your story in your copybook. Read it to a friend.

21. Write these instruments on the word ladder. Each word must begin with the
last letter of the previous word. (Look up the instruments you don't know on
www.wikipedia.org)

Ahoko
Oboe
Saxophone
Piano
Octopad
Naqara
Euphonium
Double bass
Accordion
Melodica

piano

Name a few sea creatures.

1. Read the information.

## Rays

Rays are a type of flattened fish and are closely related to sharks. They live in seas all around the world.

Unlike other fish, rays and sharks have no bones. Their skeleton is made of cartilage, like the tip of your nose.

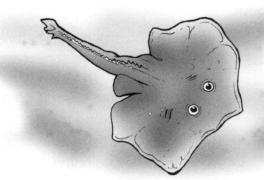

Rays look very graceful gliding like flying carpets under the water. Rays swim with a 'flying' motion, moved along by the motion of their 'wings'. They have a sleek tail with sharp spines on it. Each spine has little barbs along the edges like thorns. Their stinger is a razor-sharp spine which grows from the ray's whip-like tail. This stinger contains poison.

Some rays may be no bigger than an adult's hand while others may have a body about two metres in diameter, and including their tail, four metres in length.

Rays feed mainly on molluscs, crustaceans and small fish. Their mouths have powerful, shell-crushing teeth. They settle on the bottom while feeding, sometimes leaving only their eyes and tail visible. They hunt on or near the bottom of the ocean as they are so well camouflaged here.

It is thought that rays are intelligent creatures, even smarter than sharks. They are known to be curious, often approaching a diver and simply watching him.

The earliest known rays date from the Jurassic period, about 150 million years ago. Since rays have no bones, fossilised rays are rare, but their teeth, made of hard enamel, fossilise well.

Rays are edible and may be cooked in a similar way to other fish, grilled, battered, fried or dried.

Rays do not usually attack to defend themselves. When under threat, they often swim away. It was a sad day on 5 September 2006 when 'the Crocodile Hunter', Steve Irwin, died from a heart attack after a stingray's tail went into his chest. This happened in Australia's Great Barrier Reef. Steve Irwin had spent his life facing danger in the wild in an effort to teach the world to respect wildlife. His favourite saying was, 'Crikey!' His show, *Crocodile Hunter* was seen in more than a hundred countries and he was known to more than 500 million people. His passion and enthusiasm for all creatures made the world sit up and listen to him. Fatal attacks by rays are very rare.

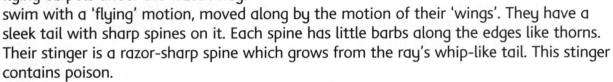

2. Talk about.

As a class, discuss what you have learnt about stingrays.
Try to remember without looking back at the text.

> In Iceland, eating pickled stingray on 23rd December
> is an old tradition.

3. Answer the questions.

a. In which seas does a ray live?

_____

b. What is its skeleton made of?

_____

c. Describe its motion under the water.

_____

d. Which part of the ray contains poison?

_____

e. What does the ray feed on?

_____

f. Why are fossilised rays rare?

_____

g. What is a tradition in Iceland?

_____

4. Answer the questions in your copybook.

a. Which sea creature is closely related to the ray?
b. Describe the ray's tail.
c. Draw a picture that shows the sizes of rays.
d. How do they camouflage themselves?
e. Why do rays' teeth fossilise well?
f. What do rays usually do if they feel threatened?
g. Are rays edible? Explain your answer.

5. In your copybook write a short newspaper article about Steve Irwin. Get your information from the text. Remember to write a headline. Write your key words here.

_____
_____
_____
_____
_____

Sometimes we shorten a word and we use an apostrophe where a letter or letters have been left out. This is called a **contraction**.

> **Sample**  **She's** in a bad mood so **don't** irritate her

6.   Write the contractions.

a.   would not   _____

b.   you have   _____

c.   you are   _____

d.   I could   _____

e.   she will   _____

f.   he is   _____

g.   do not   _____

h.   what is   _____

i.   is not   _____

j.   there is   _____

7.   Rewrite the sentences in your copybook. Use contractions to replace the underlined words.

a.   Although <u>it is</u> raining, <u>we will</u> play football.

b.   He said <u>he would</u> come to the party if he <u>was not</u> busy.

c.   <u>I have</u> got to complete my homework early as <u>we are</u> going out.

d.   <u>She is</u> my friend and <u>I will</u> do anything for her.

e.   The teacher <u>cannot</u> do the sum as <u>it is</u> too hard.

f.   <u>We have</u> done thirty minutes of exercise and <u>that is</u> enough.

g.   I think <u>I am</u> handsome and <u>you are</u> lucky to know me.

h.   Our coach <u>does not</u> think <u>we are</u> ready for the match.

i.   <u>They have</u> tidied up the classroom even though the teacher <u>did not</u> ask.

j.   <u>Who is</u> going to help me with this new game <u>I have</u> got?

8.   Underline the contractions.
Rewrite the sentences using the full form of the words.

a.   They're going to the movies but I wasn't allowed to go.

_____

b.   You needn't worry about me because I'm fine.

_____

c.   I think I'd like an MP3 player if I can't get an i-Pod.

_____

d.   Here's a gift for you because you've been working so hard.

_____

e.   They weren't singing in tune because they couldn't hear the piano.

_____

f.   I don't know what's going on in the community centre.

_____

g.   They're lucky because they don't have homework all week.

_____

h.   You should've gone to the concert as it wasn't boring at all.

_____

i.   They couldn't get into the school because it wasn't open.

_____

Plural means more than one.

> **Sample** fox – foxes

9. Underline the plural words. Rewrite the paragraph in your copybook using the singular form of the words. Be careful! Some of the other words will need to be changed too and you may have to add new words like **a**.

Parrots are colourful birds with curved bills for eating fruit and seeds, and for cracking nuts. They are noisy birds and live mostly in tropical rainforests. Parrots' feet allow them to grip branches. Cockatoos are white parrots with feathered crests on their heads.

10. Write as plurals.

| | | | | | |
|---|---|---|---|---|---|
| a. | party | _____ | k. | ferry | _____ |
| b. | wish | _____ | l. | loaf | _____ |
| c. | monkey | _____ | m. | goose | _____ |
| d. | thief | _____ | n. | teacher | _____ |
| e. | potato | _____ | o. | salmon | _____ |
| f. | echo | _____ | p. | woman | _____ |
| g. | lorry | _____ | q. | branch | _____ |
| h. | child | _____ | r. | event | _____ |
| i. | elf | _____ | s. | fly | _____ |
| j. | fish | _____ | t. | enemy | _____ |

11. Write this paragraph in plural form. Be careful! Some verbs may need to change too.

The boy was hungry. He took a walk to the restaurant. Everything looked delicious. The pizza looked cheesy. The curry looked spicy. The burger looked juicy and the chip looked crispy. He decided on a vegetable stew with a potato and a tomato. He went to sit on a bench to eat it. He had forgotten to get a knife and fork.

_____

_____

_____

_____

_____

**Word list**

| | | | | | | |
|---|---|---|---|---|---|---|
| related | unlike | skeleton | graceful | motion | visible | fossil |
| curious | edible | similar | threat | effort | favourite | passion |

12. Learn the spellings. Now look and say, picture, cover, write, check.

_____    _____

_____    _____

_____    _____

_____    _____

_____    _____

_____    _____

13. Write any words you got wrong.

_____

> I have a **passion** for relaxing.

14. Fill in the missing words. Use the word list.

  a.   If the snake feels under _____, it may bite you.

  b.   Your _____ is made up of bones.

  c.   Not all mushrooms are _____.

  d.   The swan on the lake looks _____.

  e.   My Dad has a _____ for fly fishing.

  g.   The _____ of the boat made me feel very sick.

  f.   You will need to put more _____ into your work.

15. In your copybook write your own sentences using these words:
    **fossil**, **related**, **curious**, **visible**, **similar**, **favourite** and **unlike**.

16. Answer the questions. Use the word list.

  a.   Which words from the list contain these smaller words?
       **late** _____  **eat** _____  **fort** _____  **our** _____

  b.   Write two words from the list that have a **double s**.
       _____    _____

  c.   Write a word with the suffix **ful**. _____

  d.   Write a word that has three syllables. _____

  e.   Underline a letter pattern in these words: **passion**    **motion**

  f.   Write a noun from the word list. _____

  g.   Change one letter in each to form words from the list.
       **thread** _____    **lotion** _____

  h.   Write rhyming words from the list.
       **ocean** _____    **regret** _____    **fashion** _____

## Talk about

17. Work in groups. Choose a sea creature that you would like to be. The group must guess what you are by asking questions, but you can only answer using yes or no.

## Write about

18. Write a kenning about the stingray or another sea creature. A kenning describes something familiar in an uncommon way, without using its name. The poem usually takes the form of a list, with two words on each line, often an adjective and a noun. Read the example.

**Example**

*Shark*

swift swimmer
silent predator
toothy grinner
fish gobbler
fright giver
blood sniffer
big splasher
man eater?

_____
_____
_____
_____
_____
_____
_____

(Actually, a shark will seldom attack humans.)

Write out your kenning neatly after the teacher has checked it. Display them all in the classroom.

19. How many smaller words can you find in these sea creatures? The letters must be in the same order.

> **Sample**  penguin – pen, in

a.   stingray        _____
b.   plankton        _____
c.   sailfish        _____
d.   anemone         _____
e.   pearl oyster    _____
f.   swordfish       _____
g.   sea dragon      _____
h.   mud skipper     _____
i.   coral atoll     _____
j.   hammerhead shark _____

 What images come to mind when you imagine winter?

1.   Look at the photograph.

Winter scene, Glencree, Co Wicklow

> One kind word can warm three winter months.
> *Japanese Proverb*

2.   Talk about.

As a class, think of as many winter verbs and nouns as you can. The teacher can write them on the board.

3.   Answer the questions.

a.   Where do you think this photograph might have been taken?

_____

b.   What month might it be? Explain your answer.

_____

c.   What time of day do you think it is? Explain your answer.

_____

d.   Do you think many people walk here? Explain your answer.

_____

e.  Where do you think the gate leads to?

_____

f.  What animals might be in this area?

_____

g.  Write a caption for this photograph.

_____

4.  Answer the questions.

a.  Describe the scene in three words.

_____

b.  What mood do you think the photograph depicts?

_____

c.  What can you imagine happening here?

_____

d.  What sounds might you hear if you were standing here?

_____

e.  Why do you think the photographer took this photograph?

_____

f.  Describe how you would feel if you were standing here.

_____

5.  Write a few sentences describing the scene.

_____

_____

_____

_____

6.  Write a plan for a story based on this photograph. Just write notes.

Story title: _____

Setting: _____

Plot: _____

_____

_____

Characters: _____

Beginning of the story: _____

Middle of the story: _____

Ending: _____

7. The verb **said** is used too often. Choose a verb to replace **said** and write the new sentences.

| explained | complained | shouted | whispered | promised |

a. The garda <u>said</u> to the thief that he should stop.

_____

b. The child <u>said</u> he would do his homework every day.

_____

c. The teacher <u>said</u> why the class had to be good.

_____

d. The children <u>said</u> their prayers quietly.

_____

e. The man <u>said</u> to the waiter that the food was cold.

_____

8. The verb **went** is used too often. Choose a verb to replace **went** and write the new sentences.

| hopped | crawled | waddled | marched | trotted |

a. The horse <u>went</u> around the field.

_____

b. The scared child <u>went</u> under the table.

_____

c. The rabbit <u>went</u> into the bushes.

_____

d. The soldiers <u>went</u> in front of the band.

_____

e. The duck <u>went</u> down to the river.

_____

9. The verb **got** is used too often. Choose a verb to replace **got** and write the new sentences in your copybook.

| arrived | became | arrested | received | contracted |

a. The garda <u>got</u> the thieves.
b. It <u>got</u> quite cold today.
c. The poor teacher <u>got</u> a cold.
d. They <u>got</u> home by train.
e. Lana <u>got</u> full marks for Maths.

A conjunction is a joining word. It joins words, phrases or sentences together.

> **Sample** I am not working **unless** I get paid.

Other conjunctions include: **and, as, but, so, although, if, despite, either, or, neither, nor, since, even, because**.

10. Underline and write out the conjunctions.

a. Charlie was tired so he went home. _____

b. You're not going out until your room is tidy. _____

c. I want to go cycling but my legs are sore. _____

d. You can visit me if you bring a gift. _____

e. She will write a letter or send an email. _____

f. He was tired although it was early. _____

g. She was in trouble because she forgot her homework. _____

h. Kyle was cold despite the heater nearby. _____

i. I could go to the cinema if I finish my work. _____

11. Join each pair of sentences with a conjunction from the list. Rewrite the sentences in your copybook.

> so    although    as    after    or    while    and    when    but    because

a. Anne went to bed. She watched *The Simpsons*.

b. I used an oven glove. The pan was hot.

c. Dad cleaned my room. I was sleeping.

d. We moved. I was ten years old.

e. We stayed awake. We were very tired.

f. He had no lunch. He had no dinner.

g. He was not listening to the teacher. He was distracted.

h. She had a headache. She took some medicine.

i. Brian had the ice-cream. Brian had the cake.

j. We wanted to play outside. We were not allowed to.

Try not to use the conjunctions **and** or **because** too much in your own writing. These words are overused!

I will clean my room **if** you pay me!

12. Add conjunctions to complete the sentences.

a. He will not go to the party _____ you ask him.

b. The dog was panting _____ it raced down the street.

c. I cannot go to the disco _____ I am unable to get a lift.

d. We ran around the field one more time _____ we were exhausted.

e. The teacher jumped onto a chair _____ she saw the mouse.

f. We waited inside _____ the storm was over.

g. I like milkshakes _____ I prefer water.

h. Do not be naughty _____ you could be in trouble.

i. She will go the match _____ I accompany her.

j. The boy did not win the competition _____ his best efforts.

## Word list – commonly misspelled words

| address | twelfth | occur | potato | weird | burglar | surprise |
|---------|---------|-------|--------|-------|---------|----------|
| misspell | separate | column | possess | library | vacuum | skilful |

13. Learn the spellings. Now look and say, picture, cover, write, check.

_____      _____

_____      _____

_____      _____

_____      _____

_____      _____

_____      _____

14. Write any words you got wrong.

_____

15. Fill in the missing words. Use the word list.

a. Go to your local _____ to borrow a few good books.

b. Anne is very _____ when it comes to horse riding.

c. Write your own _____ at the top of the letter.

d. The _____ was arrested by the gardai.

e. Do you _____ an English-Irish dictionary?

f. Where did the earthquake disaster _____?

g. My brother and I have _____ rooms otherwise we fight.

> Why do you want my address?

16. In your copybook write your own sentences using these words:
**twelfth**, **potato**, **weird**, **surprise**, **misspell**, **column** and **vacuum**.

17. Write the answers. Use the word list.

a. Which words end with these words?

**spell** _____  **rise** _____  **dress** _____

**rate** _____  **to** _____

b. Write the words from the list that have two syllables. _____

_____

c. Find the common letter pattern in **library**, **separate** and **burglar**.

d. Find smaller words in these words:

**address** _____  **twelfth** _____  **weird** _____  **misspell** _____

e. Write the words that start with a vowel. _____

f. Write one word that ends with a vowel. _____

g. Which letter in **column** is silent? _____

h. Write a word with double letters. _____

66

## Talk about

18. Work in a group. Act out a winter scene. It can be set anywhere, for example, camping, in the playground or playing sport.

## Write about

19. Write a winter haiku. A Haiku is a very short form of Japanese poetry using a specific number of syllables, usually seventeen. It is like a photo that captures the essence of what is happening, often connecting two unrelated things. It is often about nature and should convey emotion. You do not need to use rhyming words. Look at this example.

**Title**
5 syllables
7 syllables
5 syllables

*Winter*
Snow falling softly
Suddenly the streets are full
of laughing children

_____

_____

_____

_____

> Never dread the winter till the snow is on the blanket.
> *Irish proverb*

20. Complete the crossword.

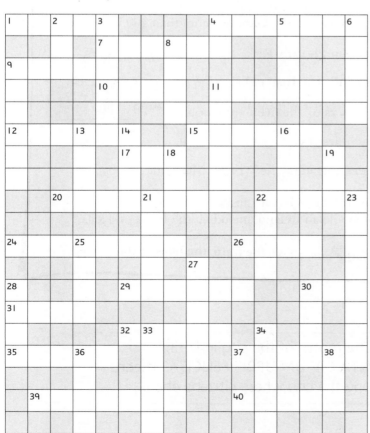

**Across:**
1. Sudden cold breeze (5)
4. Another word for 'gloves' (7)
7. Hanging spike of ice (6)
9. Freezing rain (5)
10. Present tense of 'told' (4)
11. Conditions outside (7)
12. Flowering plant, colour (6)
15. Atishoo! (6)
17. Not in (3)
20. Month of winter (8)
22. Carols etc. (5)
24. Valentine month (8)
26. Thaw (4)
29. 3 x 10 (6)
30. Small dog (3)
31. Opposite of 'dislike' (4)
32. Silky material (5)
35. Breezy (5)
37. Ice sport (6)
39. Bedtime shoe (7)
40. Direct a vehicle's course (5)

**Down:**
2. Frozen water (3)
3. Small (6)
4. Myself (2)
5. Small pie (4)
6. Neck warmer (5)
8. Chilly (4)
9. Another word for 'spade' (6)
11. A season (6)
13. Strong emotion (4)
14. Ripped (4)
16. Nought (4)
18. Bath___ (3)
19. Cloud of water vapour or mist (3)
21. Middle month of spring (5)
22. Store garden equipment here (4)
23. Road could be ___ with ice (8)
25. Be carried on (4)
27. Locomotive (5)
28. Carried along by wind (4)
30. Place with swings and slide (4)
33. Make an a__ __ el in the snow (5)
34. Wellington ___ (5)
36. Taps can do this (4)
38. You hear with this (3)

Have you been to Dublin? Maybe you live there!

1. Read the flyer.

## Welcome to Dublin
## Failte go Eire

*Enjoy yourself* in one of Europe's oldest cities!

### See some of Dublin city's many attractions:

O'Connell Bridge in O'Connell Street, named in honour of Daniel O'Connell whose statue stands nearby. Bullet holes from the 1916 Rising may be seen in this monument.

The Ha'penny Bridge, built in 1816. People were charged a half penny to cross it. It's free now!

Christchurch Cathedral, founded in 1040.

Temple Bar – with many quaint and quirky shops.

Grafton Street – non-stop shopping, and the statue of Molly Malone, about whom the song *In Dublin's Fair City* was written.

St. Stephen's Green – a beautiful inner-city park, including a garden for the blind.

The Spire – situated in O'Connell Street. It is 120m in height and was completed in January 2003. It is also called the 'Spike'.

The Four Courts – the most important courts in Ireland – the Supreme Court and the High Court sit here. Designed by architect James Gandon more than 200 years ago.

Dublin Zoo in Phoenix Park.

Restaurants and cosy Irish pubs.

Double-decker bus tours of the main attractions.

The Custom House – designed by James Gandon.

Museums and art galleries, including the Writer's Museum.

Trinity College – founded in 1592 by Queen Elizabeth of England. It houses the greatest collection of books in Ireland, including the Book of Kells.

**It's easy to get around! Choose from the bus, a taxi, the train, the Luas or the DART.**

The motto of the city in Latin:
OBEDIENTA CIVIUM URBIS FELICITAS means
'Happy the city where citizens obey.'

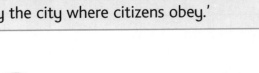

2.  Talk about.

    What different concerns might city children have compared to country children?

3.  Answer the questions.

    a.  When was Christchurch Cathedral founded?

        _____

    b.  Where will you find the statue of Molly Malone?

        _____

    c.  Where can the greatest collection of books be found?

        _____

    d.  Name a park in the city.

        _____

    e.  Which bridge did people have to pay to cross?

        _____

    f.  Who designed the Custom House?

        _____

    g.  Name two ways to travel around Dublin.

        _____

4.  Complete the sentences.

    a.  Dublin's main attraction can be seen on a _____ tour.
    b.  The Book of _____ can be found in Trinity College.
    c.  You could see African animals in _____ Park.
    d.  The song 'In Dublin's fair city' was inspired by _____.
    e.  The Supreme Court was _____ by James Gandon.
    f.  In Dublin there are many _____ and _____.
    g.  The motto of Dublin is _____.

5.  In your copybook write one sentence about each of the following.
    a.  O'Connell Street
    b.  Grafton Street
    c.  The Luas
    d.  Museum
    e.  Temple Bar

6.  Answer the questions in your copybook.
    a.  Name four animals you might see in Dublin Zoo.
    b.  Which place mentioned in the flyer interests you the most? Explain why.
    c.  Does this flyer make Dublin sound exciting? Explain your answer.
    d.  What other attraction could be added to the flyer?
    e.  If you were travelling around Dublin which form of transport would you choose?
        Give a reason for your choice.
    f.  What is special about the area or town you live in?

7. Circle the correct homophone. Rewrite the sentences in your copybook.

> **Remember** A homophone is a word that sounds the same but has a different meaning and spelling.

*I **hear** the inspector is coming **here**!*

a. She will (great / grate) more cheese onto the pizza.

b. I pulled the horse's (reins / reigns) so it would stop.

c. He was (fined / find) for not returning his library books.

d. The boys enjoyed the fight (seen / scene) in the movie.

e. The (road / rode) was slippery with ice.

f. I want to play a (board / bored) game as I am (board / bored).

g. The (witch / which) knew (witch / which) spell to create.

h. My (deer / dear) friend has (deer / dear) in the field next to his house.

i. I cannot (here / hear) the rock music from (here / hear).

j. He (knew / new) he would get a (knew / new) skateboard for Christmas.

8. Make new words by adding prefixes and/or suffixes to the root words.

a. bitter _____        k. fresh _____

b. wise _____         l. connect _____

c. proper _____       m. usual _____

d. believe _____      n. perfect _____

e. appear _____       o. please _____

f. legal _____        p. sense _____

g. lead _____         q. behave _____

h. sane _____         r. govern _____

i. agree _____        s. spell _____

j. order _____        t. possible _____

9. Rewrite the sentences in your copybook, using the shortened form of the underlined words.

a. I <u>cannot</u> go to the party if <u>I am</u> sick.

b. <u>You are</u> late and <u>I have</u> been waiting for you.

c. <u>She is</u> tired because she <u>could not</u> sleep last night.

d. <u>We are</u> going <u>General Post Office</u> if <u>it is</u> open.

e. They <u>do not</u> think <u>he will</u> win the egg and spoon race.

f. <u>You will</u> enjoy living in Orange <u>Avenue</u> next to <u>Mister</u> Plum.

g. When <u>he is</u> not writing books, <u>Professor</u> Heart lectures at <u>Dublin City University</u>.

h. <u>Doctor</u> O'Connor <u>could not</u> find anything wrong with my big toe.

i. My friend <u>is not</u> happy about going to live in the <u>United Kingdom</u> as <u>she will</u> miss all of us.

j. I <u>cannot</u> watch the programme on the <u>British Broadcasting Corporation</u> as <u>I will</u> be fast asleep.

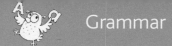

10. Add adjectives to describe the nouns. Rewrite the sentences in your copybook.

    a.    I took my radio back to the shop.
    b.    The horse trotted around the meadow.
    c.    The boy shouted and the birds flew away.
    d.    The ship sailed the sea.
    e.    The explosion damaged the building.
    f.    The children skipped to the park.
    g.    The cheetah sprinted across the plains.
    h.    The clouds gathered in the sky.
    i.    The shark seemed to be following the diver.
    j.    The hiker rested under a tree.

11. Use conjunctions to join the two sentences. Rewrite the sentences.

    a.    I like jam. I prefer Marmite.
    b.    Do not climb that wall. You will fall.
    c.    Ice the cake. Sprinkle with chocolate.
    d.    Kim will not bath. There is a bubble bath.
    e.    I will not go to bed. I am not tired.
    f.    I took off my rings. I washed my hands.
    g.    Andrew had seven dogs. Paula had only one.
    h.    You can only have dessert. You eat all your dinner.
    i.    We will throw a class party. This term is over.
    j.    He did not boast. He won five races.

12. In your copybook write these sentences in plural form. Be careful – some of the verbs will need to change too!

    a.    The pony is in the field.
    b.    The child sat on the wooden bench.
    c.    The farmer checked on the calf.
    d.    The lorry carried a big box.
    e.    The bus went through the city.
    f.    The puppy chewed on the bone.
    g.    The lady washed the glass.
    h.    The man was working on the machine.
    i.    The sheep was quietly grazing in the meadow.
    j.    The monkey was swinging on the branch.

13. List some items that you would find more than one of in the classroom.

_____
_____
_____
_____
_____
_____

**Word list**

| important | honour | statue | including | cathedral | written | college |
|---|---|---|---|---|---|---|
| collection | designed | museums | galleries | attractions | cosy | oldest |

14. Learn the spellings. Now look and say, picture, cover, write, check.

_____     _____

_____     _____

_____     _____

_____     _____

_____     _____

_____     _____

15. Write any words you got wrong.

_____

16. Fill in the missing words. Use the word list.

a. Jemma has a large _____ of teddy bears.

b. Beautiful artwork hangs in _____ around Ireland.

c. Do you know who _____ the Eiffel Tower in Paris?

d. There are many tourist _____ in Ireland.

e. It is warm and _____ by the fire.

f. The total amount for the meal is €20, _____ the tip.

g. After you have finished school, you can study at _____.

*Galleries are not places for that sort of thing! Out you go!*

17. In your copybook write your own sentences with these words:

**important**, **honour**, **statue**, **cathedral**, **written**, **museums** and **oldest**.

18. Write the answers. Use the word list.

a. Write the root words.

**collection** _____ **designed** _____ **oldest** _____

**galleries** _____ **attractions** _____

b. Underline the silent letters in **designed** and **honour**.

c. Write a word from the list that is in plural form. _____

d. Which words from the list contain these smaller words?

**act** _____ **the** _____ **our** _____

**leg** _____ **import** _____

e. Underline the letter pattern that is the same in **collection** and **attractions**.

f. Write a word with a **soft g**. _____

g. Write a word that is a noun. _____

h. Write a word from the list that starts with a vowel. _____

## Talk about

19.  Work in a group to make a television advertisement for Dublin city.
     Make it sound wonderful! Present your advertisement to the class.

## Write about

20   Write a flyer to advertise your school. Focus on all the positive aspects and make your school sound attractive.

> Think about:
> ● Where is your school?
> ● What are names of the teachers?
> ● What facilities does your school have?
> ● What activities does your school provide?
> ● What sports are played in your school?
> ● What is your school's motto?
> ● What is special about your school?
> Make your flyer eye-catching and interesting.

21.  Type out your flyer neatly and add pictures.
     Display the flyers in the school.

> The River Liffey divides Dublin into north and south.

22.  Follow the directions.

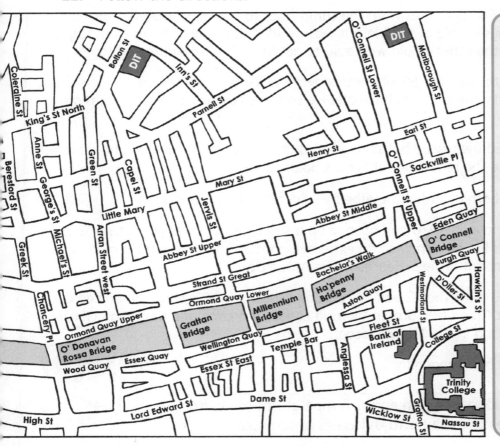

1.  Start in Coleraine Street and go south. Turn left into King Street North.
2.  Take the 3rd turning right into Green Street.
3.  Keep going straight into Aaron Street East.
4.  Turn left into Ormond Quay Lower.
5.  Walk straight – do not cross the Millennium Bridge.
6.  Turn right and go over the Ha'penny Bridge.
7.  Turn left into Aston Quay.
8.  Turn right into Westmorland Street.
9.  Pass right by the Bank of Ireland on your right.
10. Cross over the road into Grafton Street.
11. Look for the entrance of the college on the left.

What is the name of the college?

What is an explorer?

1.  Read the text.

## Tom Crean

Tom Crean was an Irish Antarctic explorer. He was born in the town of Annascaul in Co. Kerry in 1877. In 1892 he joined the Royal Navy, lying about his age to get in.

Tom Crean was on three of the four major expeditions to Antarctica:

- Discovery (1901–1904)
- Terra Nova (1911–1913) – led by Robert Scott
- Endurance (1914–1816) – led by Ernest Shackleton

Tom Crean

### Terra Nova

Crean, Lashly and Evans were the last support party to leave Scott on his way to the South Pole. While Scott continued on, these men turned back 268km from the pole on 4th January 1912. They faced a 1206km journey back to the camp.

Around the beginning of February, and 160 kilometres from the camp, Evans became seriously ill with scurvy. Crean and Lashly had to pull him on a sledge, as he was unable to walk. This was slowing them down considerably and they were running out of food. Evans kept asking to be left behind but Crean and Lashly refused.

When they were about 56 kilometres from the camp (four to five days' travel), they had between one to two days supply of food left. It was decided that one of them would stay behind with Evans and the other would walk solo to get help. Crean volunteered to get help.

It took Crean 18 hours to walk the 56 kilometres over the ice to reach the camp. He did this only eating three biscuits and a bit of chocolate. He collapsed on arrival – at 3.30am on February 19.

A severe blizzard delayed the rescue but finally Evans and Lashly were rescued and returned to the camp alive, unlike the remainder of Scott's polar party.

Crean and Lashly were both awarded the Albert Medal for saving Evans' life.

Crean retired from the navy in 1920 and opened up a small pub in Kerry called *The South Pole Inn.* Throughout his life he remained an extremely modest man. He put his medals away and never spoke about his experiences in the Antarctic.

There are other amazing feats that Crean has accomplished and he is commemorated in at least two places: Mount Crean (2550m) in Victoria Land, Antarctica and the Crean Glacier in South Georgia, an island in the Atlantic ocean.

He died in 1938 from a burst appendix.

> Antarctica is the coldest place on earth. Temperatures range from
> –85 degrees C in winter to 0 degrees in summer.

2. Talk about.

Would you be brave enough to be an explorer?
What special qualities are needed to be an explorer?

3. Answer the questions.

a. Where was Tom Crean born?

_____

b. Name one major expedition to Antarctica.

_____

c. How far did Crean, Lashly and Evans have to travel back to the camp?

_____

d. What slowed down their journey?

_____

e. Write a sentence about Crean's solo journey.

_____

f. What did Crean do when he retired in 1920?

_____

g. Name one place that is named after Tom Crean.

_____

4. Answer **yes** or **no**. Explain your answers in your copybook.

a. Evans could not make the journey on foot.           _____
b. Crean did not boast about his accomplishments.       _____
c. Evans and Lashly were rescued immediately.           _____
d. Crean did not have much food for his solo journey.   _____
e. Crean and Lashly were not recognised for their bravery. _____
f. Crean arrived at the camp during the night.          _____
g. Tom Crean went on two major expeditions to Antarctica. _____

5. In your copybook write the meaning of each word:

a. explorer          c. scurvy          e. blizzard
b. expedition        d. volunteered     f. modest

6. Write your own sentence using one or more of the words from question five.

_____

7. Answer the questions in your copybook.

a. Describe Tom Crean's character.
b. Why do you think Tom Crean wanted to explore the Antartic?
c. What kind of things do you think the men took with them on the expedition?
d. If you were an explorer where would you like to go?

**Two** means the number 2.

| Sample | I have **two** pillows. |

**To** can be a preposition or an adverb.

| Sample | I want **to** go **to** bed. |

**Too** means also or very.

| Sample | This work is **too** easy. I want to go home **too**. |

8.  Complete the sentences using **to**, **too** or **two**. Rewrite the sentences in your copybook.

    a.    I went _____ the shed _____ get the shovel.

    b.    I think I have had _____ much tea today.

    c.    Helen wants _____ buy _____ hamsters.

    d    My little brother is going _____ the disco _____ .

    e.    We can go _____ the playground at _____ -thirty.

    f.    I find this classroom _____ noisy _____ work in.

    g.    My Mum wrote a letter _____ the teacher _____ ask if I could leave early.

    h.    My dog wants _____ go swimming _____ .

The word **done** never follows a noun or pronoun. It is usually accompanied with **have** or **had** unless at the end of a sentence.

| Sample | I **done** my work. (X) I **did** my work (✓) or I **have done** my work. |

9.  Complete the sentences using **done** or **did**. Rewrite the sentences in your copybook.

    a.    I have _____ all my work so neatly.

    b.    Jack _____ the crossword puzzle in the newspaper.

    c.    Simon _____ all the shopping yesterday.

    d.    Hester has _____ very good work today.

    e.    They have _____ all their tests for the term.

    f.    She _____ all her chores before she left the house.

    g.    The class _____ very good work and the teacher is pleased.

    h.    My aunt has _____ the marathon and she received a medal.

**Its** means belonging to something.

| Sample | The cat is biting **its** tail. |

**It's** means **it is** or **it has**.

| Sample | **It's** been snowing. |

10. Complete the sentences using **its** or **it's**. Rewrite the sentences in your copybook.

    a.    The cat is sleeping in _____ basket.

    b.    _____ a pity that today is Monday.

    c.    The monster ate all _____ dinner.

    d.    My dog thinks _____ a sheep. It likes to eat grass and it won't touch _____ dog food.

    e.    We just bought a new TV. _____ brilliant and _____ even got surround sound.

    f.    The cat went to sleep in _____ basket with _____ kittens.

    g.    The stew has lost _____ flavour because _____ been cooked for too long.

Synonyms are words that mean the same thing.

Sample  small – little

11. Match the synonyms.

Please can you give us a **tiny**, **miniscule**, **teensy-weensy** bit of homework?

| | | |
|---|---|---|
| a. | difficult | plentiful |
| b. | sad | dangerous |
| c. | right | yearly |
| d. | cold | friend |
| e. | nasty | hard |
| f. | abundant | scared |
| g. | brave | buy |
| h. | rapid | correct |
| i. | option | unkind |
| j. | strong | freezing |
| k. | annually | quick |
| l. | fearful | powerful |
| m. | pal | unhappy |
| n. | perilous | choice |
| o. | purchase | heroic |

12. Rewrite the paragraph in your copybook using synonyms for the underlined words.

| gobbled | delicious | full | began | huge | pile | slice | finished | starving |
|---|---|---|---|---|---|---|---|---|

Monty was <u>hungry</u>. He <u>started</u> with a <u>big</u> piece of cheese. Then he <u>ate</u> a <u>piece</u> of pizza. He <u>ended</u> with a <u>stack</u> of <u>tasty</u> pancakes and jam. Then he felt <u>stuffed</u>.

13. Rewrite the paragraph in your copybook using different synonyms.

14. Write synonyms for the underlined words. Rewrite the sentences in your copybook.

a.  My neighbour's car is <u>fast</u> and <u>expensive</u>.

   _____   _____

b.  I am so thrilled that today is <u>warm</u> and <u>bright</u>.

   _____   _____

c.  The game we played was <u>hard</u> and <u>exhausting</u>.

   _____   _____

d.  In the battle the soldier was <u>brave</u> and <u>strong</u>.

   _____   _____

e.  Aiden's schoolbag was <u>big</u> and a <u>strange</u> colour.

   _____   _____

f.  Please be <u>quick</u> at the shop and do not stop to <u>chat</u> to <u>friends</u>.

   _____   _____

**Word list**

| | | | | | | |
|---|---|---|---|---|---|---|
| explorer | major | lying | kilometres | journey | beginning | unable |
| refused | severe | chocolate | arrival | alive | modest | medals | amazing |

15. Learn the spellings. Now look and say, picture, cover, write, check.

_____  _____
_____  _____
_____  _____
_____  _____
_____  _____
_____  _____
_____  _____
_____

16. Write any words you got wrong.

_____

17. Fill in the missing words. Use the word list.

a. On _____ at the airport, our cousins called us to collect them.
b. The distance from the school to my house is five _____.
c. For my birthday I would like a _____ cake.
d. The _____ storm wreaked havoc on the town.
e. It is a long _____ from Ireland to Australia.
f. The boys won _____ for their football skills.
g. The teacher _____ to let me go home.
h. My Mum is _____ to take me to the fair.

School is amazing!

18. In your copybook write your own sentences using these words:
**alive**, **lying**, **amazing**, **explorer**, **major**, **beginning** and **modest**.

19. Answer the questions. Use the word list.

a. Write the root words of these words from the list.
**explorer** _____ **unable** _____ **lying** _____
**beginning** _____ **arrival** _____
b. Which words from the list have these endings?
**ate** _____ **used** _____ **or** _____
c. Underline the suffixes in **amazing** and **refused**.
d. How many words have three syllables? _____
e. Write two words ending in **ing**. _____ _____
f. Write two nouns from the list. _____ _____
g. How many words from the list begin with a vowel? _____

## Talk about

20. Work in pairs. Imagine the scene where Evans is asking to be left behind and Crean and Lashly are refusing. Act out the scene.

## Write about

21. In your copybook write a speech honouring Tom Crean, or another brave person, for their heroic deeds. Write your key words here.

22. Work in groups. Deliver your speech to the group.

There is a bronze statue of Tom Crean in Annascaul.

23. Work out the coded names of polar explorers.

| A | B | C | D | E | F | G | H | I | J | K | L | M |
|---|---|---|---|---|---|---|---|---|---|---|---|---|
| ✡ | ✛ | ✜ | ♣ | ✤ | ◆ | ◇ | ★ | ☆ | ✪ | ✫ | ✬ | ✭ |
| N | O | P | Q | R | S | T | U | V | W | X | Y | Z |
| ✮ | ✯ | ✰ | ✱ | ✲ | ✳ | ✴ | ✵ | ✶ | ✷ | ✸ | ✹ | ✺ |

_____

_____

_____

_____

_____

Roald Amundsen       Otto Schmidt       Ernest Henry Shackleton

Robert Falcon Scott       Henry Hudson

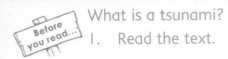
What is a tsunami?

1.  Read the text.

Tsunami, Sri Lanka, 26.12.2004

## *Tsunami*

The 2004 Indian Ocean Earthquake was an undersea earthquake that occurred on 26 December 2004.

The earthquake triggered a series of tsunamis that spread throughout the Indian Ocean. These had devastating effects across South and Southeast Asia, including Indonesia, Sri Lanka, India and Thailand. The most recent figures show a loss of 229,866 people. 42,883 of these are missing. This disaster, known as the Asian Tsunami, is one of the worst disasters in modern history.

The magnitude of the earthquake was between 9.1 and 9.3 on the Richter Scale. It lasted between 500 and 600 seconds. It was so strong that it caused the whole planet to vibrate and move at least more than one centimetre. It also triggered earthquakes in other locations as far away as Alaska.

With waves up to 30 metres, the destruction was vast. The furthest death recorded caused by the disaster was in Port Elizabeth, South Africa, which is 8000km away from the epicentre.

Somehow, many animals seemed to know danger was ahead. Many people reported seeing animals fleeing for higher ground minutes before the tsunami arrived. Very few animal bodies were found, suggesting that many of them did escape the danger. Wildlife experts believe that an animal's acute hearing and other senses might enable it to hear or feel the Earth's vibration.

What is a tsunami? A tsunami is a series of waves, and the first wave may not be the most dangerous. A tsunami 'wave train' (one after another) may come five minutes to an hour apart. Sometimes there is a retreat of the ocean. Some people who saw this retreat on that disastrous day knew what it meant and fled to higher ground. Some who were fascinated by the retreat of water ran closer to take a look.

The whole world responded to the disaster and US$7 billion was raised to help those affected by the earthquake.

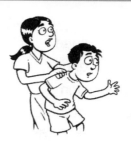

2. Talk about.

As a class, talk about the after effects of such a disaster. How would children who survived be affected?

> Look at the Richter scale on this website:
> http://en.wikipedia.org/wiki/Richter_scale

3. Answer the questions in your copybook.
   a. When did the Indian Ocean Earthquake occur?
   b. What did the earthquake trigger?
   c. Name three countries that were affected.
   d. What was the magnitude of the earthquake?
   e. How long did the earthquake last?
   f. What is a tsunami?
   g. How much money was raised?

4. Complete the sentences.
   a. The Indian Ocean Earthquake is also known as _____.
   b. The earthquake occurred _____ the sea.
   c. The earth _____ at least more than one centimetre.
   d. Waves were as _____ as 30 metres.
   e. People reported that they _____ animals flee for higher ground before the tsunami arrived.
   f. A wave train is _____.
   g. Some people who were fascinated by the water _____ ran to get a closer look.

5. In your copybook write the meanings of these words. Use your dictionary.
   a. series          c. magnitude        e. epicentre
   b. devastating     d. locations        f. acute

6. Write your own sentence using one of the words from question five.

   _____

7. Answer the questions in your copybook.
   a. Did you see coverage of this tsunami on the television? Describe what you saw.
   b. How would the survivors have been affected by the tsunami?
   c. How would the tsunami still be affecting people today?
   d. How could you help people who have been affected by disasters?

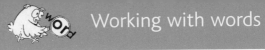
8. Underline the silent letters.

a. knee          f. comb          k. half
b. gnaw          g. wrench        l. ghost
c. sign          h. hymn          m. cupboard
d. island        i. build         n. debt
e. rhubarb       j. answer        o. iron

> The wren jumped on the wrought iron gate.

9. Write the missing letters and then the complete sentences.

| w | k | l | b |

a. The plum___er might ___now why the loo is leaking.

_____

b. My feet are num___ from wa___king in the snow.

_____

c. All this ___nitting hurts my ___rists.

_____

d. The ___night in armour had a fine s___ord.

_____

e. I dou___t Batman will ta___k to me.

_____

10. Sort the words by their silent letters.

| receipt | solemn | scent | gnat | column | raspberry |
| scissors | autumn | science | design | psalm | gnome |

| Silent c | Silent g | Silent n | Silent p |
|----------|----------|----------|----------|
|          |          |          |          |
|          |          |          |          |
|          |          |          |          |

11. Write six sentences using words with silent letters.

_____

_____

_____

_____

_____

_____

Adverbs tell us more about the verb.

> **Sample** He talked **slowly**.

To change an adjective into an adverb, we often add **ly**.

12. Underline the adverbs.

The moon shone brightly. The young boy walked quickly along the darkened lane. He was breathing heavily. He looked around him nervously. He could imagine monsters glaring at him hungrily. He started to sprint hurriedly towards home. At last, he made it safely to the front door. He turned the handle silently and stepped carefully inside. He saw a shape moving menacingly towards him. It was only his grandmother creeping silently down the stairs.

13. Change the words into adverbs.

|   |   |   |   |   |   |
|---|---|---|---|---|---|
| a. | sweet | _____ | k. | sad | _____ |
| b. | silent | _____ | l. | sleepy | _____ |
| c. | angry | _____ | m. | proud | _____ |
| d. | loud | _____ | n. | nasty | _____ |
| e. | happy | _____ | o. | tired | _____ |
| f. | famous | _____ | p. | fortunate | _____ |
| g. | unkind | _____ | q. | rare | _____ |
| h. | weary | _____ | r. | simple | _____ |
| i. | heavy | _____ | s. | serious | _____ |
| j. | quiet | _____ | t. | beautiful | _____ |

14. Complete the sentences with suitable adverbs.

a. The child ate the pasta _____.

b. The school choir sang _____.

c. The teacher shouted _____.

d. Jack did his homework _____.

e. The lion stared _____ at me.

f. The swans moved _____ across the lake.

g. The leopard crept _____ through the bush.

h. The train went _____ through the stations.

i. The class did their projects _____.

j. Clutching her list, she shopped _____.

> I can **easily** beat you.

15. Add adverbs to complete the sentence about yourself.

I am sitting _____ and working _____.

**Word list**

| modern | series | planet | worst | throughout | effects | recent | locations |
| caused | experts | disaster | tsunami | centimetre | enable | responded |

16. Learn the spellings. Now look and say, picture, cover, write, check.

_____          _____
_____          _____
_____          _____
_____          _____
_____          _____
_____          _____
_____

17. Write any words you got wrong.

_____

18. Fill in the missing words. Use the word list.

    a.  A bicycle will _____ me to get from place to place.
    b.  _____ tell us that sleep is very important for our health.
    c.  There is a feeling of happiness _____ the school.
    d.  I like watching the 'Blue Planet' television _____.
    e.  Ken _____ to the letter by making a phone call.
    f.  Ten millimetres is equal to one _____.
    g.  The earthquake had devastating _____.
    h.  Mars is a _____ in the solar system.

> How can I escape?

19. In your copybook write your own sentences using these words:
    **modern**, **recent**, **locations**, **caused**, **disaster**, **tsunami** and **worst**.

20. Write the answers. Use the word list.

    a.  Write a word from the list that has a **soft c**. _____
    b.  Break **throughout** into two words. _____ _____
    c.  Which words from the list contain these smaller words?
        **used** _____ **pond** _____ **sun** _____
    d.  Which word has the most syllables? _____
    e.  Write a word from the list that is in plural form. _____
    f.  How many words from the list begin with a vowel? _____
    g.  Underline the suffixes:  **caused    responded**
    h.  Which word from the list contains the 24ᵗʰ letter of the alphabet?
        _____

**Talk about**

21. Work in pairs. Prepare a news report on the Indian Ocean Earthquake. Practise it, taking turns to read. Present your news report to the class.

**Write about**

22. Choose a charity and research it. Design a poster for the charity that will encourage people to donate money. Include some information about the charity on your poster. Do a rough draft first.

> Think about:
> ● What is the name of the charity?
> ● Who do they help?
> ● How do they use the donations?
> ● How could you contact them?

> The MMS Scale is also used now to measure earthquakes. Read up on it!

23. Check your work then write or type out your poster neatly. Display the posters in school.

24. On the map match the natural disasters with arrows to their country of location. Use a detailed world map to help you.

1. The Yellow River Flood – China (1931) (+–850,000 –4,000,000 died)
2. Volcanic eruptions – Nevado del Ruiz, Columbia (1985) (+–23,000 died)
3. Earthquake and tsunami, Messina, Italy (1908) (+–70,000 died)
4. Chicago, USA heatwave (1995) (+–739 died)
5. Rains and mudslides, Venezuela (1999) (+–15,000 died)
6. Tangshan Earthquake, China (1976) (+–255,000 died)
7. Hurricane Katrina, USA (2005) (1836 died, 705 are missing)
8. Bangladesh Cyclone (1991) (+–138,000 died)
9. Irish Potato Famine (1845–1849) (+–1,100,000 died)
10. Great smog of 1952, United Kingdom (+–4000 died)

When might you write a letter of complaint?

1. Read the letter of complaint.

15 Sweet Street
Tiny Town
15 November 2007

The Manager
Bob's Bistro
20 Sour Street
Tiny Town

## RE: Food and service in your restaurant

Dear Mr. Jackson,

My birthday was on 20 May and my parents kindly took me out to celebrate this special occasion. I was looking forward to an evening of fine dining and we chose your restaurant. However, we were very disappointed and my birthday was completely ruined.

On arrival we were ushered to a table which was sticky and had some greasy blobs on it. We mentioned this to the waiter who looked very irritated that he should have to wipe it down. My chair was so wobbly I felt seasick. I had to stick napkins under the legs to keep myself steady. The background music was not suitable for an evening meal. I do not mind heavy metal at a rock concert but not for a quiet night out.

We ordered our food and waited, and waited, and waited. With all the time it took you would have thought it would have been good. My father's chicken was cold and my pasta was hard and chewy. There seemed to be a few black things in the sauce which I could not identify. My poor mother choked on her piece of fish, which was raw. Luckily, my father was on hand to help her.

We tried once again to complain, but the waiter informed us the manager could not be disturbed as he was upstairs watching his favourite TV programme. Then as if we hadn't suffered enough, the waiter knocked my orange juice into my lap. I am not sure if this was intentional.

The worst insult was being presented with the bill. When my father informed the waiter that we would not pay for such bad service and food, he was threatened with the gardaí.

The correct thing for you to do would be to apologise to our family and reimburse the money we spent. I hope that we can solve this matter in an amicable way. In the meantime, I suggest that you improve the services in your restaurant.

I look forward to hearing from you.

Yours sincerely,

*Gerard Simpson*

Gerard Simpson

2. Talk about.

Do you think Gerard Simpson was right to complain? What would you have done?

3. Answer the questions.

a. What is the name of the restaurant?

_____

b. How many people went to dinner?

_____

c. What was the attitude of the waiter?

_____

d. What music was playing in the background?

_____

e. What was Gerard drinking?

_____

f. Where was the manager?

_____

g. What does Gerard want the manager to do?

_____

Do not forget quotation marks.

4. In your copybook quote from the story to prove the statements. (You do not have to write full sentences.)

a. The chairs were not comfortable.
b. The food took a long time to arrive.
c. The family were celebrating a special day.
d. The mother's meal was not properly cooked.
e. The waiter expected them to pay the bill.
f. The evening was not a success.
g. Mr. Simpson wants his money back.

5. In your copybook, write the meanings of these words. Use your dictionary.

a. ruined       c. heavy metal     e. intentional     g. apologise
b. ushered      d. identify        f. insult          h. amicable

6. Write your own sentence using one or more words from question five.

_____

7. Answer the questions in your copybook.

a. What do you think was the worst thing that happened in the restaurant?
b. Is the tone of the letter friendly or unfriendly? Explain.
c. What do you think the manager should have done?
d. Write about a restaurant experience you have had.

When adding a suffix to a word sometimes the last letter of the word has to be doubled.

> **Sample** rob + ed = ro**bb**ed, mad + er = ma**dd**er

8.  Word sums. Follow the rule about doubling the last letter.

a.  swim + ing = _____
b.  wet + er = _____
c.  flat + en = _____
d.  chop + ing = _____
e.  hot + est = _____
f.  nap + ing = _____
g.  begin + ing = _____
h.  flip + ing = _____

i.  bat + ed = _____
j.  wag + ing = _____
k.  stop + ed = _____
l.  shop + er = _____
m.  hug + able = _____
n.  trap + ed = _____
o.  fit + er = _____
p.  trim + er = _____

When adding a suffix to a word ending in **e**, we usually drop the **e** before adding the suffix.
If the first letter of the suffix is a consonant, we usually keep the **e**.

> **Sample** hope – hopeful

> **Sample** have – having

> My dog is **taking** me for a walk.

9.  Word sums. Follow the rules about words ending in **e**.

a.  hope + less = _____
b.  slope + ing = _____
c.  complete + ly = _____
d.  taste + less = _____
e.  approve + ing = _____
f.  stare + ing = _____
g.  slide + ing = _____
h.  judge + ment = _____

i.  drive + ing = _____
j.  nice + er = _____
k.  manage + ment = _____
l.  decorate + ing = _____
m.  rotate + ed = _____
n.  breath + less = _____
o.  grumble + ed = _____
p.  shake + en = _____

When adding a suffix to a word ending in **y**, sometimes the **y** changes to an **i**.
When adding **ing** we keep the **y**.

> **Sample** hurry – hurrying

> **Sample** hurry – hurried

> I am **carrying** the cake.

10.  Word sums. Follow the rules about words ending in **y**.

a.  happy + ly = _____
b.  deny + ed = _____
c.  grumpy + er = _____
d.  bully + ing = _____
e.  pity + ful = _____
f.  worry + ing = _____
g.  lazy + ness = _____
h.  fancy + ed = _____

i.  silly + ness = _____
j.  study + ing = _____
k.  delay + ed = _____
l.  try + ed = _____
m.  penny + less = _____
n.  hurry + ed = _____
o.  lucky + ly = _____
p.  deny + ed = _____

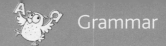

Verb tenses are important because they tell you when things happened.

> **Present tense:** She eats curried beans on toast. (It is happening now.)
> **Past tense:** She ate curried beans on toast. (It has happened.)
> **Future tense:** She will eat curried beans on toast. (It will happen)

11. In your copybook write the sentences in the future tense. (The words **will** and **shall** are often used in the future tense.)

   a. Our football team was beaten yesterday.
   b. Alan waits for his Mum to collect him.
   c. Rita had a fantastic birthday party.
   d. I stood at the bus stop for twenty minutes.
   e. The rain beats hard against the window.
   f. I cleaned out the rabbit hutch.
   g. The man wrote a letter of complaint to the manager.
   h. Chris caught a butterfly but he set it free.
   i. Dad slept on the couch with the television blaring.
   j. The tractor went by and splashed her with mud.

> **Take note:**
> It is the verb that changes with the tenses.

12. In your copybook write the sentences in the past tense.

   a. Carol eats fish pie for dinner.
   b. The children run around the field.
   c. Brendan catches fish in the local stream.
   d. I creep up on my brother to scare him.
   e. The water in the lake freezes.
   f. When the doorbell rings, I always answer it.
   g. The shop is open and it sells CDs and DVDs.
   h. I catch salmon and bring it home for dinner.
   i. Joe sees a flying saucer but I do not see anything.
   j. We meet new people when we go to drama class.

13. In your copybook write the sentences in the present tense.

   a. The canary sang beautifully.
   b. The teacher taught us how to behave.
   c. I cleaned and tidied my room.
   d. The dog suddenly stopped and panted.
   e. The buildings shook and wobbled during the earthquake.
   f. She was nervous when she stood up to talk.
   g. They swam in the lake when it was sunny.
   h. Humpty fell off the wall and broke into small pieces.
   i. My Mum told me that she felt excited about my match.
   j. The school took us to the ballet and we thoroughly enjoyed it.

> Always stick to one tense in a piece of writing.

**Word list**

| | | | | |
|---|---|---|---|---|
| manager | complaint | evening | ruined | background |
| suitable | luckily | disturbed | programme | insult |
| gardaí | spent | solve | meantime | improve |

14. Learn the spellings. Now look and say, picture, cover, write, check.

_____     _____
_____     _____
_____     _____
_____     _____
_____     _____
_____     _____
_____

15. Write any words you got wrong.

_____

16. Fill in the missing words. Use the word list.

    a. The detectives were confident they would _____ the crime.
    b. I do not think those orange spotty trousers are _____.
    c. Make a _____ if you are unhappy about a service.
    d. If you _____ someone it will hurt their feelings.
    e. I know that you could _____ your handwriting.
    f. Jackie loves to watch a music _____.
    g. The _____ is in charge of the shop.
    h. The owner of the house _____ the robber.

We are trying to **solve** the mystery of the missing **hampster!**

17. In your copybook write your own sentences using these words:
    **evening, ruined, background, luckily, gardaí, spent** and **meantime**.

18. Write the answers. Use the word list.

    a. Write a compound word from the list. _____
    b. Write two words from the list that have an **ai** pattern.

       _____    _____

    c. Find smaller words in these: **complaint** _____
       **suitable** _____ **spent** _____ **improve** _____
    d. Write a word with double letters. _____
    e. Write a verb from the list. _____
    f. Write a word that has a **soft g**. _____
    g. Write a word that has a **silent e**. _____

## Talk about

19. Work in pairs to act out a scene between a diner and a waiter. The diner should complain about the food and service. The waiter should try to calm the situation and make the diner happy!

## Write about

20 Write a letter of complaint. Follow the format of the letter at the beginning of this unit. Check your letter, write or type it out neatly. Read out your letter to the class.

> Tips for writing a formal letter:
> - Use formal language. Do not use abbreviations, slang words or contractions.
> - Do not use exclamation marks.
> - Include your own address and the company's address.
> - If you don't know the name of the person, then use Dear Sir / Madam.
> - Begin with a brief description of what the letter is about and underline it:
> **RE: Poor food and service**
> - End with *Yours sincerely*. If you have used Dear Sir / Madam, then use *Yours faithfully*.
> - Use paragraphs.
> - Try to use the best words so that your letter sounds professional.

21. A waiter has written down an order using his own form of shorthand. Can you understand it?

_____

_____

_____

_____

_____

_____

> *2 bgrs – 1 ches*
> *Steak – MR, mush sau*
> *Cod, msh*
> *Rst lmb, veg, no pot*
> *3 chip – 1 curr*
> *2 ckn nug.*
> *1 spag. bol*
> *3 milksh – 2 choc, 1 straw*
> *5 wtr*

22. Write this food order in your own shorthand.

2 chicken burgers and chips; 1 bacon burger, no chips; fish and curry chips; steak – well done with salad and cheese sauce; beef curry and rice; vegetable soup; 2 sausages and mash, one with gravy; roast pork with roast potatoes and vegetables; 1 garlic bread; portion of onion rings

_____

_____

_____

_____

_____

Before you read...

Do you believe in ghosts?

1.  Read the poem.

## *The ghost teacher*

The school is closed, the children gone,
But the ghost of a teacher lingers on.
As the daylight fades, as the daytime ends,
As the night draws in and the dark descends,
She stands in the classroom, as clear as glass.
And calls the names of her absent class.

The school is shut, the children grown,
But the ghost of the teacher, all alone,
Puts the date on the board and moves about
(As the night draws on and the stars come out)
Between the desks – a glow in the gloom –
And calls for quiet in the silent room.

The school is a ruin, the children fled,
But the ghost of the teacher, long-time dead,
As the moon comes up and the first owls glide,
Puts on her coat and steps outside.
In the moonlit playground, shadow-free,
She stands on duty with a cup of tea.

The school is forgotten – children forget –
But the ghost of a teacher lingers yet.
As the night creeps up to the edge of the day,
She tidies the Plasticine away;
Counts the scissors – a shimmer of glass –
And says, 'Off you go!' to her absent class.

She utters the words that no one hears,
Picks up her bag ...
                    and
                        disappears.

*Allan Ahlberg*

Temple Michael in Cork is said to be haunted.
People have reported hearing screams and have seen moving lights.

Leap Castle in Co. Offaly is said to be the most haunted place
in Ireland. Many people have seen the top windows suddenly
light up as if many candles were in the room.

2.  Talk about.

Discuss the poem with the class. Do you like the poem?

3.  Answer the questions.

a.  When does the ghost teacher come out?

_____

b.  What is the first thing the teacher does?

_____

c.  What does she do in the playground?

_____

d.  Why is the class 'absent'?

_____

e.  What does she write on the board?

_____

f.  What does she do with the scissors?

_____

g.  Which birds are mentioned in the poem?

_____

4.  In your copybook quote from the poem to prove the statements.
    (You do not have to write full sentences.)
    a.  The ghost teacher is transparent.
    b.  The pupils she taught are much older now.
    c.  There is no-one else in the school.
    d.  The teacher doesn't stand still in the classroom.
    e.  She leaves before it is morning.
    f.  She dismisses the class before she leaves.
    g.  No one is listening to her.

5   In your copybook write the meanings of these words. Use your dictionary.
    a.  lingers          c.  gloom          e.  glide          g.  utters
    b.  descends         d.  ruin           f.  shimmer

6.  Answer the questions in your copybook.
    a.  Do you think the school is still being used? Explain your answer.
    b.  Why do you think the ghost teacher goes to the school?
    c.  What kind of teacher do you think the ghost teacher was?
    d.  What is the mood of the poem?
    e.  Where do you think she goes when she disappears?

Alliteration is when two or more words start with the same consonant sound.

> **Sample** **K**evin **c**rept **c**arefully into the **k**itchen **c**upboard.

Take note! Alliteration means the same sounds, not letters.

7. Underline the letters that create alliteration.

   a. The maniacal man made mulberry and maple muffins.
   b. Susie says that snakes are sweet when swallowed.
   c. I think Paul put my pen into his pocket.
   d. The dark doorway filled me with dread.
   e. The big, black book is by the blue bench.
   f. I would like cucumber, carrot and kipper curry.
   g. When you wash, wash well.
   h. Bill will bite you if you break his bike.
   i. Phil fetched Fred from the funny farm.
   j. Colm gave Cáit a kiss for Christmas.

The teacher was terribly tired today.

8. Fill in the spaces with words that alliterate the underlined ones.
   Use a dictionary to help you. Your sentences can be silly!

   a. <u>Paula picked</u> a _____.
   b. <u>Wendy wished</u> she <u>would win</u> a _____.
   c. <u>Killian's cupcake</u> was covered in _____.
   d. <u>Silly Sally said</u> she <u>saw</u> a _____.
   e. <u>Chad chased</u> the _____.
   f. <u>Tod</u> wants two _____.
   g. The jolly giant _____.
   h. <u>Ron</u> the <u>wrestler</u> _____.

9. Choose three letter sounds and write a sentence for each using alliteration.

   a. Sound 1: _____
   b. Sound 2: _____
   c. Sound 3: _____

10. Try to say this tongue twister.

> *Peter Piper picked a peck of pickled peppers*
> Peter Piper picked a peck of pickled peppers
> A peck of pickled peppers Peter Piper picked;
> If Peter Piper picked a peck of pickled peppers,
> Where's the peck of pickled peppers Peter Piper picked?

Pronouns are used in place of nouns.

> **Sample** Gavin went to the doctor as **he** felt ill.

11. Circle the correct pronoun. Underline the other pronouns in each sentence.

    a. Cian's dog had puppies and now he must find good homes for (them / they).

    b. He wanted more pizza but (me / I) didn't give him any.

    c. It was bitterly cold so (we / us) all wore scarves and hats.

    d. Jeremy has his own room which (him / he) tidies every day.

    e. Both (her / she) and the teacher went to the principal's office.

    f. With (who / whom) did you go to the restaurant?

    g. Ann was feeling unwell so (she / her) went home.

    h. The teacher asked (me / I) to sit still and be quiet.

    i. The boys were bored so (them / they) decided to build a go-cart.

    j. I hope that you and (me / I) can be best friends.

12. Replace the nouns in brackets with the correct pronouns.

    a. (Spain) _____ is a popular place to go to in the summer.

    b. (Al) _____ met (Rose and Kerry) _____ after school and (Al, Rose, Kerry) _____ went to the shop.

    c. (Mum and I) _____ bought a toy for the dog but (the toy) _____ was too hard.

    d. (Derek) _____ let (Bronwyn) _____ stroke the cat and (the cat) _____ purred.

    e. (The boys) _____ asked (Shannon and I) _____ out on a date.

    f. (Bronagh) _____ told (Derek) _____ a funny joke and (Derek) _____ could not stop laughing.

    g. (My cousin and I) _____ went with (Paul and Clair) _____ to pick up litter in the town.

    h. (The day) _____ is raining so (the teachers) _____ won't make us run today.

13. Complete the sentences using suitable pronouns. (There may be more than one option.)

    a. My Mum and _____ like to feed the ducks by the river.

    b. _____ has been raining for two weeks now.

    c. _____ can swim in that cold water but _____ will not.

    d. Jenny will give Deon a card because she likes _____.

    e. Are you the boy _____ has a pet lizard?

    f. I do not know anything about _____.

    g. Vegetables are good for you so you should eat _____ every day.

    h. You are not as handsome as _____ am.

    i. These colourful runners are _____ and those dull ones are _____.

    j. Fran brushes _____ cat's fur every day so _____ coat stays shiny.

**Word list**

| | | | | |
|---|---|---|---|---|
| ghost | daylight | descends | classroom | absent |
| gloom | clear | playground | duty | forgotten |
| tidies | lingers | shimmer | utters | disappears |

14. Learn the spellings. Now look and say, picture, cover, write, check.

_____     _____
_____     _____
_____     _____
_____     _____
_____     _____
_____     _____
_____     _____
_____

15. Write any words you got wrong.

_____

16. Fill in the missing words. Use the word list.

a. You should have a good reason for being _____ from school.

b. During _____ hours most nocturnal animals will sleep.

c. The smell of my brother's deodorant _____ in the air.

d. It is your _____ to report any bullying in the school.

e. The cable car _____ from the top of the mountain.

f. There are swings and a slide in the _____.

g. The class never _____ a word during tests.

h. A good child _____ up after himself.

> The monster under my bed **disappears** during the day.

17. In your copybook write your own sentences using these words:
**classroom**, **ghost**, **shimmer**, **clear**, **gloom**, **forgotten** and **disappears**.

18. Write the answers. Use the word list.

a. Write a compound word from the list. _____

b. Write the root words of these:

   **forgotten** _____  **tidies** _____  **disappears** _____

c. Which words from the list contain these smaller words?

   **him** _____  **ends** _____  **sent** _____

d. Underline the silent letter in **descends**, **ghost** and **daylight**.

e. Underline the letter pattern that is the same in:  **gloom**  **classroom**

f. In your copybook write words from the list that rhyme with the list words.

g. Write a verb from the list. _____

## Talk about

19. Work in pairs to recite the poem *The ghost teacher*. Make the poem sound spooky by changing your tone of voice and facial expressions.

## Write about

20. Imagine you are going to make lunch for your teacher. Make a list of really funny or revolting foods that you'll be serving. In your copybook turn your list into a rhyming poem.

**Example**

I'd dish up heaps of rice covered in glue,
Or slices of mouldy bread, all green and blue.

Write your list of foods here.

_____
_____
_____
_____
_____
_____
_____
_____

21. The answers to these questions all begin with the letter **b** and feature in school. The number refers to how many letters there are in each word.

a. A kind of pen (9) _____

b. Covering for windows (6) _____

c. Talk very quickly (6) _____

d. The teacher writes on this (10) _____

e. A conjunction meaning **as** (7) _____

f. Where books are kept (9) _____

g. Your sandwich is made from this (5) _____

h. The school building could be built from these (6) _____

i. A sudden bright idea (9) _____

j. Something on your jumper that may show the school crest (5) _____

k. Throw your litter in here (3) _____

l. More than one person could sit on this (5) _____

m. You may use this to show where you have read up to (8)

_____

n. You don't come to school on this day (Hint: banks are closed on this day.) (4, 7) _____ _____

o. Another word for 'capital' letters (5) _____ letters

Media photographers

Do you like to have your photograph taken?

1.  Look at the photograph.

| Saying: One picture is worth a thousand words. |

2.  Talk about.

Who is your hero or heroine? Tell the class and give reasons for your choice. Is this person often photographed?

3.  Answer the questions.

a.  How many photographers can you see? _____

b.  Who or what might they be photographing? _____

c.  Why would it be important for them to get a good photo? _____
_____

d.  Where might this be taking place? _____

e.  What can you see in the background? _____

f.  Do the photographers have ordinary cameras? Explain your answer. _____
_____

g.  Write a new caption for this photograph. _____
_____

4. Answer the questions.

a. What kind of weather do you think it is? Explain your answer.

_____

b. Why might there be a garda standing by?

_____

c. What facial expression does the man on the left-hand side have?

_____

d. Do you think the photographers co-operate with each other? Explain your answer.

_____

e. Do you think these photographers would be called 'paparazzi'? Explain your answer.

_____

f. Imagine you were the person being photographed. How might it make you feel?

_____

g. If you were a photographer, what subject would you like to photograph?

_____

Paparazzi is a term used for freelance photographers who take photos of celebrities.

5. Write five possible headlines for the photos that are being taken.

_____
_____
_____
_____
_____

6. Imagine you are a photographer waiting hours to photograph a celebrity. Say who you are waiting for and how you are feeling.

_____
_____
_____
_____
_____
_____
_____

7.  Circle the correct word in brackets. Rewrite the sentences in your copybook.

    a.   Please (weight / wait) for me to finish my lunch.
    b.   Do not (alter / altar) your story as it is excellent.
    c.   The (current / currant) in the sea will sweep you away.
    d.   My mother (scent / sent) me to buy teabags.
    e.   The car engine has a (cereal / serial) number.
    f.   The (principle / principal) gave the children a stern warning.
    g.   You have (groan / grown) so much taller this year.
    h.   I love to go to the (beach / beech) to feel the sand between my toes.
    i.   The (fowl / foul) has black, brown and red feathers.
    j.   The canal boat was tied up at the (key / quay).

8.  Word sums. Remember the rules!

    a.   snip + ing =  _____        i.   write + er =  _____
    b.   excite + ing =  _____      j.   cry + ed =  _____
    c.   funny + est =  _____       k.   care + less =  _____
    d.   forgot + en =  _____       l.   marry + ing =  _____
    e.   greedy + ly =  _____       m.   beauty + ful =  _____
    f.   take + ing =  _____        n.   freeze + ing =  _____
    g.   bury + ed =  _____         o.   tune + ful =  _____
    h.   thought + less =  _____    p.   regret + ed =  _____

9.  Write the root word. Write a second word that can be formed from the same root word.

| | Root word | Second word |
|---|---|---|
| undoes | | |
| disagreement | | |
| playfully | | |
| leadership | | |
| returnable | | |
| additional | | |
| discomfort | | |
| employer | | |
| lovelier | | |
| carefully | | |
| unusual | | |
| electrical | | |
| actress | | |
| excitable | | |
| decided | | |

10. In your copybook rewrite the sentences adding speech marks, commas, capital letters, aspostrophes, question marks and full stops.

   a. of course you have to complete all the work replied miss reilly

   b. the mcgovern family are boating on the river shannon this august said nathan

   c. please read cinderella to me begged my sister diane

   d. when ive tidied my room im going to relax and watch tv said theo

   e. my room is full of posters music magazines board games reading books and teddy bears remarked benjamin

   f. tom explained im late because i burnt my toast

   g. enda asked does this shirt look good on me

   h. emily is getting an i-pod whispered fiona

   i. i saw a mouse in the classroom said brenda

   j. dr donald said you have quite a bad cough so i think you should stay at home for a few days

11. In your copybook write the sentences in the past tense.

   a. They write letters to their girlfriends and seal them with a kiss.

   b. He buys new pens and pencils for school.

   c. She sleeps with four blankets to keep her warm.

   d. The cat drinks warm milk from a saucer.

   e. The thief steals my CDs and runs away.

   f. I try to get all my spellings right but I find them difficult.

   g. She sings loudly in the shower and we laugh at her.

   h. My Mum flips the pancakes and they land on the floor.

   i. I think my brother is acting a little crazy.

   j. My Dad creeps around the house and gives me frights.

Miss Muffet sat on her tuffet.

12. Select a pronoun to complete the sentence. (Some sentences have more than one option.)

   a. The puppies snuggled up to their mother. _____ were warm and cosy.

   b. Stan is trying to bake cookies but _____ is just making a mess.

   c. My MP3 player is very old. _____ hardly works.

   d. Roger and I have saved some money. _____ are buying a skating ramp.

   e. Maggie received many gifts. It was _____ birthday.

   f. My work looks untidy. _____ looks so neat.

   g. There was no soap so Brendan washed _____ with shampoo.

   h. The children are excited because _____ are leaving school early.

   i. The lady asked _____ for directions to get to the school.

   j. You cannot have any of my biscuits because they are all _____.

**Word list – Commonly misspelled words**

| | | | | | | | |
|---|---|---|---|---|---|---|---|
| amend | height | miniature | withhold | truly | extreme | gauge | eighth |
| vehicle | niece | average | rhyme | calendar | grammar | foreign | |

13. Learn the spellings. Now look and say, picture, cover, write, check.

_____   _____
_____   _____
_____   _____
_____   _____
_____   _____
_____   _____
_____

14. Write any words you got wrong.

_____

15. Fill in the missing words. Use the word list.

   a.   We need to get _____ currency before we travel abroad.

   b.   The pupil was _____ sorry for forgetting her homework.

   c.   I came _____ in the race and I am proud of myself.

   d.   The rain _____ showed that it had rained heavily.

   e.   Make a note of my birthday on your _____.

   f.   My sister's daughter is my _____.

   g.   *Little Boy Blue* is a nursery _____.

   h.   Snowboarding and bungee-jumping are considered
        to be _____ sports.

> You have turned writing into an **extreme** sport.

16. In your copybook write your own sentences using these words:
    **miniature**, **height**, **amend**, **withhold**, **average**, **grammar**
    and **vehicle**.

17. Write the answers. Use the word list.

   a.   Write the root words of these words:
        **amend** _____ **height** _____ **truly** _____

   b.   Which words from the list contain these smaller words?
        **me** _____ **age** _____ **reign** _____

   c.   Break this word into two words: **withhold** _____ _____

   d.   How many 3-syllable words are there? _____

   e.   Write a word from the list that has a **soft g**. _____

   f.   Underline the silent letters in **gauge**, **vehicle**, **miniature** and **foreign**.

   g.   In your copybook write the last eight words in alphabetical order.

## Talk about

18. Work in pairs. One person plays a famous celebrity and the other is a reporter. The reporter asks questions in a friendly and professional manner. The celebrity can make up the answers.

## Write about

19. In your copybook write a newspaper article about someone you admire, or about an event.

> Tips for writing a newspaper article:
> - Write the headline (title at the top of the newspaper article).
> - Use formal language – no contractions, abbreviations or slang.
> - Give details such as names, dates and places.
> - Use correct grammar and punctuation.
> - Read newspaper articles to see how it is done.

20. Write the key words for your article here.

_____

_____

_____

_____

21. These are actual newspaper headlines. Rewrite them in your copybook so that they make more sense.

   a. POLICE BEGIN CAMPAIGN TO RUN DOWN JAYWALKERS
   b. MILK DRINKERS ARE TURNING TO POWDER
   c. SAFETY EXPERTS SAY SCHOOL BUS PASSENGERS SHOULD BE BELTED
   d. QUARTER OF A MILLION CHINESE LIVE ON WATER
   e. EYE DROPS OFF SHELF
   f. LAWMEN FROM MEXICO BARBECUE GUESTS
   g. TWO SISTERS REUNITE AFTER EIGHTEEN YEARS AT CHECKOUT COUNTER
   h. INCLUDE YOUR CHILDREN WHEN BAKING COOKIES
   i. DRUNKS GET NINE MONTHS IN VIOLIN CASE
   j. STOLEN PAINTING FOUND BY TREE
   k. RED TAPE HOLDS UP NEW BRIDGES
   l. CHEF THROWS HIS HEART INTO HELPING FEED NEEDY
   m. HOSPITALS ARE SUED BY SEVEN FOOT DOCTORS

How many saints can you name?

1.   Read the story of St. Brendan.

## St. Brendan

St. Brendan was probably born in the year 484
near Ardfert in Co. Kerry. He grew up to be an
important monk and then an abbot. He founded
monasteries in Ardfert and in other parts of Ireland.

Brendan was a great sailor and people called him Brendan the Navigator. There are
many stories, poems and songs that tell of Brendan's long sea voyage to North America
in the 6th century. The story tells how Brendan and seventeen monks sailed to a faraway
land in a boat covered with oxhides. If this is true, it means that St. Brendan reached
America 400 years before the Vikings, who were supposed to have been the first. Many
do not believe that St. Brendan made this voyage while others are convinced he did.

In the 1970s an explorer called Tim Severin built an ox leather curragh and re-enacted the
voyage as described in the stories. The boat was made exactly how it would have been for
St. Brendan, and took almost three years to build. Severin left Kerry on 17 May 1976. It
took him two summers to sail from Ireland, via the Hebrides, Faroe Islands and Iceland to
Newfoundland. He did this to demonstrate that the saint's voyage was possible.

The stories about St. Brendan's voyage tell how the saint and his monks made a picnic
on an island. They settled down on the island and started a fire, with which to cook their
meat. Then suddenly the island started to move! The monks fled back to their boat in
fear and watched as the 'island' swam away. St. Brendan told them it was a whale, one
of the largest sea creatures. Tim Severin encountered many whales on his journey. Many
of these whales liked to come up close to the leather boat.

Halfway between Scotland and Iceland lie the eighteen islands which are called the
Faroes. The stories of St. Brendan also tell of how the saint and his monks landed at a
place called the Island of Sheep. According to the stories, huge white sheep were
everywhere. The word 'faroe' is a Viking word that means 'sheep island'. To this day, the
sheep on these islands are very big and also, very white.

In the stories, it tells of how the men sailed past the Island of Fire, off the southern coast
of Iceland. It was said that people threw burning rocks at their boat and it looked like the
whole island was on fire. Iceland is famous for its volcanoes, some on land, and others
rising up out of the sea. Maybe this is what the monks had seen – flames, steam and
burning rocks thrown into the air by a volcano.

In stories, St. Brendan sees a huge 'pillar of bright crystal'. When Tim Severin and his
crew were on the last stage of their journey, they saw icebergs drifting by every day.

Tim Severin and his crew covered nearly 6400 kilometres of the Atlantic Ocean. They
arrived at their destination on 26 June 1977. They proved that St. Brendan could have
reached North America 1500 years ago, but no one really knows if he did. What do you
think?

2.  Talk about.

    If St. Brendan and the monks had made this journey, what hardships do you think they may have encountered?

3.  Answer the questions.

    a.  When and where was St. Brendan born?

    _____

    b.  Why was he called 'Brendan the Navigator'?

    _____

    c.  Where was St. Brendan supposed to have travelled to?

    _____

    d.  What did Tim Severin do?

    _____

    e.  What was Tim Severin trying to prove?

    _____

    f.  Describe what happened when they picnicked on an island?

    _____

    g.  What are the Faroes?

    _____

    h.  How far did Tim Severin and his crew travel?

    _____

4.  Answer the questions. Write the answers in your copybook.
    a.  What was St. Brendan's profession?
    b.  Write a sentence about the boat St. Brendan used.
    c.  What route did Severin take?
    d.  What is special about the sheep on the Island of Sheep?
    e.  Why do you think the island they passed was called the Island of Fire?
    f.  What could the 'pillars of bright crystals' seen by St. Brendan have been?
    g.  Exactly how many days did it take Severin to complete the journey?
    h.  Do you think St. Brendan made this journey? Explain your answer.

5.  In your copybook write words from the story with the same meaning as these.
    a.  journey
    b.  come across
    c.  landing-place
    d.  a mountain formed by volcanic material
    e.  houses or places where monks live
    f.  a large, floating mass of ice
    g.  show, prove
    h.  a boat with a wooden frame, over which is stretched animal skins or hides

6.  Write your own sentence using one or more words from question five.

    _____

7.  In your copybook write the sentences using the full forms of the words.

    a.  She doesn't need cake as she's just had biscuits.

    b.  Sheila can't go swimming because she hasn't got her swimsuit.

    c.  I'll go with you to the match if you'll come with me to the ballet.

    d.  He hasn't telephoned to say he'd be late.

    e.  You needn't be concerned about your test because I'm sure you will do well.

    f.  Mona says she's tired and she should've gone to bed earlier.

    g.  You've come first in every race and they're proud of you.

    h.  Dara couldn't phone me last night as he's got no credit.

    i.  Don't worry, if you didn't do it, you will not be in trouble.

    j.  There's so much work to do and I haven't even started.

8.  Underline the common letter pattern in each line. Write two more words with the same letter pattern.

    a.  around, astound, bound        _____  _____

    b.  height, weight, sleigh        _____  _____

    c.  bought, thought, trough       _____  _____

    d.  flight, tightly, brightening  _____  _____

    e.  flatten, tent, tender         _____  _____

    f.  your, rumour, flour           _____  _____

    g.  slice, police, office         _____  _____

    h.  beware, scare, glare          _____  _____

    i.  wealthy, deaf, jealous        _____  _____

    j.  chair, hairy, flair           _____  _____

9.  Add prefixes and/or suffixes.

    a.  visit        _____

    b.  understand   _____

    c.  solve        _____

    d.  post         _____

    e.  effect       _____

    f.  true         _____

    g.  form         _____

    h.  depend       _____

    i.  child        _____

    j.  equal        _____

    k.  add          _____

    l.  port         _____

    m.  restrict     _____

    n.  believe      _____

    o.  safe         _____

You have made a **mess**! I cannot believe you can be so **messy**! I will not stand for this **messiness**!

10. Underline the punctuation mistakes. Rewrite the paragraph correctly in your copybook.

frogs are amphibians which means they live on land and in water most frogs catch moving insects by darting out their long sticky tongues

frogs begin life as tadpoles hatching in the water from eggs called spawn after 7 to 10 weeks tadpoles grow legs and lungs and they develop into frogs

what noise does the largest frog in the world make it makes no sound at all the three-foot long goliath frog from central africa is mute there are 4,360 species of frog but only one of them goes 'ribbit' this frog is the pacific tree frog that lives in hollywood frogs make a huge variety of noises they croak snore grunt cluck chirp and growl the barking tree frog yaps like a dog and a frog from south america grunts like a pig female frogs are mostly silent

11. Write an adjective and an adverb that can be formed from these nouns.

| | Adjective | Adverb |
|---|---|---|
| hunger | | |
| loudness | | |
| skill | | |
| anger | | |
| beauty | | |
| silence | | |
| sadness | | |
| intelligence | | |
| nervousness | | |
| warmth | | |

12. Complete the sentences with suitable prepositions. Rewrite the sentences in your copybook.

a. The remote control is _____ the cushion.

b. I have to rely _____ my charm when I ask my Mum for something.

c. My little brother seems to get the blame _____ everything.

d. Your handwriting is similar _____ mine.

e. The teacher was filled _____ joy when she read our lovely stories.

f. She will meet him _____ the shop _____ the bank.

g. Our football team played _____ our rivals and we beat them _____ a point.

h. They went _____ the supermarket and bought tubs _____ ice-cream.

i. The boys jumped _____ the gate and _____ the stream.

j. They sailed _____ the coast _____ a small yacht.

**Word list**

| | | | | |
|---|---|---|---|---|
| probably | sailor | voyage | century | proved |
| exactly | possible | covered | according | island |
| southern | volcanoes | crystal | pillar | Viking |

13. Learn the spellings. Now look and say, picture, cover, write, check.

_____          _____
_____          _____
_____          _____
_____          _____
_____          _____
_____          _____
_____          _____
_____

14. Write any words you got wrong.

_____

15. Fill in the missing words. Use the word list.

   a. My little brother was _____ in mud from head to toe.
   b. You should always do _____ as the teacher tells you.
   c. _____ to my mother, I am a very special child.
   d. You will _____ get all these sentences correct.
   e. Waterford is famous for its _____ glass.
   f. One hundred years is called a _____.
   g. Australia is in the _____ hemisphere.
   h. Red hot lava can flow from _____.

> I wish I was on a deserted **island** right now.

16. In your copybook write your own sentences using these words:
   **sailor**, **voyage**, **possible**, **Viking**, **island**, **proved** and **pillar**.

17. Write the answers. Use the word list.

   a. Write a word from the list that has a **soft c**. _____
   b. Underline the silent letter in **island**.
   c. Find smaller words in these words:
      **probably** _____ **voyage** _____ **crystal** _____
   d. Write the root of these words:
      **sailor** _____ **southern** _____ **covered** _____
   e. How many words from the list have three syllables? _____
   f. In your copybook write the last eight list words in alphabetical order.

## Talk about

18. Work in groups. Tell the group whether or not you think St. Brendan made this voyage. Explain your answer and try to convince the group that you are right.

## Write about

19. Imagine you are St. Brendan on his voyage. In your copybook write a diary entry for one day. Put everyone's diary entries together in a class booklet. Remember: A diary entry is written in the first person: 'I ...' Do your rough work here.

In 1994 the Faroe Islands issued a stamp in memory of the travels of St Brendan.

20. Create an Irish saints wordsearch. Get a friend to do your wordsearch.

**Irish saints:**
- Brendan
- Mogue
- Fergal
- Sanctan
- Davnet
- Erc
- Berach
- Flannan
- Gobain
- Cyra
- Macartan
- Ceallach
- Malachy
- Otteran
- Laserian

Carroll Education Limited
34A Lavery Avenue
Park West Industrial Estate
Nangor Road
Dublin 12

http://www.carrolleducation.ie

Copyright © Janna Tiearney 2007
Commissioning Editor: Helen Dowling
Managing Editor: Maggie Greaney
Publishing Consultant: Gay Judge
Designer: Derry Dillon
Print Origination: Design Image
Illustrator: Derry Dillon

First published May 2007. Reprinted 2008. This reprint May 2009.

ISBN: 978-1-84450-093-2

Photo acknowledgements:
Imagefile Ireland: p 8 (Hoffmann's Two-toed Sloth), p 80 (Tsunami, Sri Lanka, 26.12.2004)
Dominic Ledwidge-O'Reilly: p 62 (Winter scene, Glencree, Co Wicklow), p 98 (Media photographers)
Royal Geographical Society Picture Library: p 74 (Tom Crean)

Faroe Islands postage stamp use by permission of the publishers Postverk Føroya hat.

Every effort has been made to trace copyright holders but we would be glad to rectify any omissions at the next reprint.